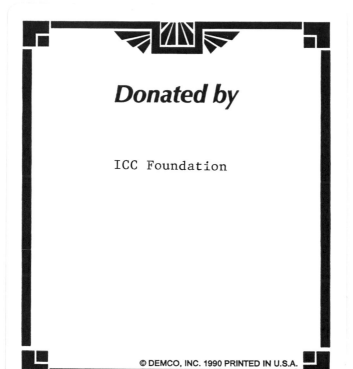

PRAISE FOR *MEGACOMMUNITIES*

"Transforming health is one of the most critical challenges—and important opportunities—facing America today. Over the past two years we've used Booz Allen's "megacommunity" model to address both pandemic influenza and Alzheimer's disease—two particularly difficult cases. In both instances, the results were powerful and far-reaching. Simply put, these concepts work. We'll be applying the methods explained in this important book even more ambitiously in the months ahead."
> —*Newt Gingrich, former Speaker of the U.S. House of Representatives,*
> *founder of the Center for Health Transformation*

"This book provides a much-needed new perspective on leadership in a networked environment, demonstrating clearly and concisely the value of a "leader of leaders." This is a must-read for managers and aspiring leaders."
> —*Fulvio Conti, chief executive officer, Enel*

"*Megacommunities* offers a comprehensive, groundbreaking approach to the challenge of global interdependence. An eminently readable and practical handbook for everyone interested in shaping a future of sustainable progress and social inclusiveness, *Megacommunities* deserves the widest possible audience. This is one of those rare well-reasoned books that can make a real difference in the world."
> —*Richard D. Parsons, chairman of the board and CEO, Time Warner*

"*Megacommunities* presents a timely framework for developing multifaceted and self-reinforcing solutions to the problems of the twenty-first century. As the authors describe, our largest problems can be turned into profitable solutions when we focus on optimization rather than maximization. Creating these responsive solutions, therefore, requires the substitution of brainpower for dogma. . . . The authors accurately find that progress is well underway, and that we are indeed self-selecting integrated approaches for the inherent benefits that they bring. For those seeking insight on dynamic and resilient problem solving, *Megacommunities* provides a rich foundation to help accelerate the evolution of a healthier and more equitable world."
> —*Amory B. Lovins, chairman and chief scientist, Rocky Mountain Institute*

"*Megacommunities* is a problem-solving action manual for the twenty-first century. It is essential reading for leaders in business, government and civil society who are addressing some of the toughest societal challenges locally and globally. The authors provide us with a groundbreaking model that has the power to change the world for the better."
> —*Melanne Verveer, co-founder and chairman, Vital Voices Global Partnership*

"An insightful and engrossing read, *Megacommunities* brings creative new thinking to the challenges confronting leaders in our increasingly complex and interdependent world. It addresses problems head on, is full of good sense, and offers guidance that is compelling. This important book, for the strategist in particular, is hard to ignore."
> —*Admiral Sir Ian Forbes (Ret.), former NATO Supreme Commander*

"*Megacommunities* introduces us to a world of complex problems, where traditional economic and financial incentives are not sufficient, where it is impossible for all players to secure their first choice outcome. And where multiple vetoes operate and free riders abound. This world calls for creativity and imagination, the ability to build trust, form alliances and do deals. Megacommunities also provokes a rethink about how we identify and develop our political, business and civic leaders—people who can think across the boundaries of their own organizations, can communicate, can influence and be influenced, who think in terms of optimizing rather than maximizing, and who, in short, can pilot us from the selfish world of the Prisoner's Dilemma to the collaborative world of John Nash's Equilibrium."
> —*Lord Andrew Turnbull, former UK Cabinet Secretary and Head of the Civil Service*

"As the new President and CEO of Common Cause, an organization that works to ensure that the political process serves the public interest, I wholeheartedly agree that progress in business, government and civil society must be attained through citizen-centered multi-lateral solutions. In our near 40-year history of reform work, Common Cause has long believed that engaging a diverse citizenry as well as a wide array of coalition partners is the most effective path to significant change, and *Megacommunities* captures that well."
> —*Dr. Robert W. Edgar, President and CEO, Common Cause*

"*Megacommunities* offers unique insight about how modern leaders can deal with the growing challenges and complexities of our globalizing world. The authors give valuable, common sense advice about how to maneuver large organizations and big ideas through an increasingly networked, connected, more complicated global society. Any serious leader in business, government and civil society needs to read this work and apply its lessons."

—*General John Abizaid (Ret.), United States Army and former Commander of the United States Central Command*

"As the modern world has become more interdependent and global, the magnitude and complexity of the problems facing society have also grown. The ability to manage highly dispersed people and operations while responding to unusual problems and crises requires new tools and new leadership approaches. This important and incisive book illuminates how the mutual self-interests of actors in private, public and non-governmental organizations can be harnessed to develop shared approaches to dealing with very complex challenges in such disparate areas as economic strength, national security or broad health or environmental issues. The Booz Allen authors's concept of 'megacommunities' as an organizing principle for managing collaboratively across traditional functional boundaries—and thereby transitioning from a hierarchal management structure to one characterized by networks of networks of experts—has wide applicability. It is a critical new tool for today's leaders—and tomorrow's."

—*Denis A. Bovin, Vice Chairman, Investment Banking, Bear, Stearns & Co. Inc.*

"For too long 'public-private partnerships' to solve global problems have left out the majority of the public—the four billion poor of the developing world. 'Megacommunities' is a bold and big idea that will give the poor an equal voice in global efforts to deal with what they know best—poverty."

—*Hernando de Soto, president, Instituto Libertad y Democracia, Perú and author of* The Mystery of Capital

"When really big problems come knocking, including natural disasters, epidemic diseases or the slower moving dislocations of globalization or environmental degradation, you had better hope you can call upon the resources of a healthy, vibrant megacommunity. Complex problems cannot be addressed by government, business or civil society acting alone. *Megacommunities* offers pragmatic advice, born from case studies and the broad experience of many leaders, on how to join civil society and the commercial and public sector behind resolution of challenges that none can meet alone."

—*Curt Struble, Former U.S. Ambassador to Peru*

"*Megacommunities* offers a refreshing, organizational framework to help leaders solve the thorny and complex problems that devolve from technology and globalization. The book elaborates the networked strength of collaboration between business, government and civil society."

—*Richard H.K. Vietor, Senator John Heinz Professor of Environmental Management, Harvard Graduate School of Business Administration*

"The complex issues of today's world have finally a strategic solution. The post globalized world calls for tri-sector leaders to acknowledge how the traditional sphere of influence and competences have changed and conflicts are even more complex that anyone can do it alone. *Megacommunities* cuts through the complexity with precise path to leadership."

—*Andrea Ragnetti, member of the Board of Management of Royal Philips Electronics and CEO of Philips Consumer Lifestyle Sector*

"Geocomplexity, network capital, dynamic tension, swarm intelligence—this is the language of Megacommunities. But unlike so many other books promising management miracles, these terms are not old ideas in new jargon. They outline a genuinely different framework for thinking about the world and its multiplying problems. Best of all, they become actual tools for tackling those problems. This book is a ray of hope!"

—*Anne-Marie Slaughter, Dean of the Woodrow Wilson School of Public and International Affairs at Princeton University*

MEGACOMMUNITIES

HOW LEADERS OF GOVERNMENT, BUSINESS AND NON-PROFITS CAN TACKLE TODAY'S GLOBAL CHALLENGES TOGETHER

Mark Gerencser
Christopher Kelly
Fernando Napolitano
Reginald Van Lee

palgrave
macmillan

MEGACOMMUNITIES
Copyright © Booz Allen Hamilton, Inc.

First published in 2008 by
PALGRAVE MACMILLAN™
175 Fifth Avenue, New York, N.Y. 10010 and
Houndmills, Basingstoke, Hampshire, England RG21 6XS.
Companies and representatives throughout the world.

PALGRAVE MACMILLAN is the global academic imprint of the Palgrave
Macmillan division of St. Martin's Press, LLC and of Palgrave Macmillan Ltd.
Macmillan® is a registered trademark in the United States, United Kingdom
and other countries. Palgrave is a registered trademark in the European
Union and other countries.

ISBN–13: 978–0–230–60398–1
ISBN–10: 0–230–60398–X

Library of Congress Cataloging-in-Publication Data
Megacommunities : how business, government, and civil society leaders can
master this century's global challenges together / Mark Gerencser . . . [et al.].
    p. cm.
  ISBN 0–230–60398–X (alk. paper)
  1. Leadership. 2. Social action. I. Gerencser, Mark.
  HM1261.M44 2008
  303.48'4—dc22

A catalogue record of the book is available from the British Library.

Design by Letra Libre

First edition: March 2008
10 9 8 7 6 5 4 3 2 1
Printed in the United States of America.

CONTENTS

FOREWORD

n his 1943 book, *Physics and Philosophy*, Sir James Jeans told us that our thinking regarding ideas "usually advances by a succession of small steps, through a fog in which even the most keen-sighted explorer can seldom see more than a few steps ahead. Occasionally the fog lifts, an eminence is gained, and a wider stretch of territory can be surveyed—sometimes with startling results." In the wake of a big idea—one capable of lifting the fog that we have been operating in—we don't see the world in quite the same way anymore. Our approach to thinking about an issue gets rearranged. Perspectives shift, fragments of ideas fit together in ways we didn't think about previously. All this can come from an idea—one that is not a small step, but rather a big leap!

Ideas of this type are rare, but when they appear on the scene they certainly make themselves known. Megacommunities will undoubtedly become one of these ideas. And it couldn't come at a more appropriate time.

We are all in desperate need of game-changing ideas. Why? The simple answer is that we face a growing list of complex and challenging issues, and as a society we increasingly find ourselves stuck. Not necessarily for a lack of trying, or for a lack of appreciation of the consequences. We know that these issues—global climate change, preparing for pandemics, responding to natural disasters, global terrorism, water scarcity, aging populations, aging infrastructure, to name but a few—have the potential to become massive challenges in the next few years. And these problems manifest on both global and local levels. Consider how the need to develop new anti-terrorism or antipandemic initiatives applies not just globally but city by city, or how new levels of natural disasters—and new drains on government resources—can lead to situations like the one experienced in Biloxi, Mississippi or New Orleans since Hurricane Katrina.

These issues are the "Gordian knots" of our time—we can see them clearly, but they don't seem to have any clear solution. Unfortunately, we cannot cleave them in two and call it quits. We need to attempt to solve them. But the dynamic nature of the issues makes top-down, command-and-control, and reductionist management methods ineffective. Instead, this situation calls for innovative, integrative, and holistic leadership approaches.

In this book, the authors introduce us to just such an approach—the megacommunity approach. They present a new way of thinking—a big idea—that promotes and supports mutual leadership. Their approach brings decision-makers from the three sectors—government, business, and civil society—together to actively address shared issues. The concepts contained in this book are quite timely, because the ability to act decisively in the face of new complexities is fast becoming a major priority for leaders in the three sectors.

These new complexities are a natural consequence of a world made smaller by greater integration and interdependency. Issues that arise in this environment can abruptly and unpredictably escalate, with a scale and magnitude that can quickly overwhelm the effected institutions. As a result, leaders from all three sectors face a growing need to operate in a more open, distributed, and collaborative manner that recognizes the shared nature of risks, rewards, and responsibility. Unfortunately, this type of activity is not intuitive for most leaders.

This book will help readers embrace this new style of leadership—one that is as effective at facilitating cooperation among leaders in other sectors and organizations as it is within one's own organization. And it will help leaders realize that the megacommunity lessons learned can be applied at every level of tri-sector interaction, from the most international to the most narrowly-targeted community level.

I first began working with Booz Allen Hamilton, a global strategy and technology consulting firm, in 2004 when it was featured in the first Aspen Ideas Festival. In a panel session titled "Malignant and Malevolent Threats: Dealing with Potential Disasters both Natural and Terrorist-Planned," we explored how threats such as these have acquired a new urgency in our "globalized" world. The increasing movement of people, capital, and ideas across national borders has brought with it new vulnerabilities. The discussion focused on the fact that these threats cannot be dealt with entirely as a problem of corporate strategy, operations and governance, or through legislation and regulation alone. Pan-global events such as SARS, the 9/11 terrorist attacks, and the tsunami in South Asia helped raised our awareness about the economic and societal consequences of a world that has grown more connected. Yet globalization contains a very intriguing paradox: The more interdependent we become, the more we require order.

In attempting to deal with this paradox, we find ourselves facing a very complex situation. New levels of complexity, then, are really at the heart of the challenges we all face today as leaders. Dealing with complexity is a long standing and ongoing role of leaders in business and government, but dealing with complexity on this scale introduces new challenges. Our challenge—and the challenge that this book tackles—is one that is on everyone's mind: What can leaders do to more effectively confront the complexity in the world today? Our panel in 2004 explored this question, and set many of us off on a new vector related to global complexity.

In 2005, we expanded this issue at the Ideas Festival into a track of its own, called Global Dynamics. This is the term my colleagues at Booz Allen use to capture a new way of thinking about issues which focuses as much on understanding the complexity of the issue, as it does on solving it. The panels in the Global Dynamics Track focus on new ways of making sense of the complexity surrounding these issues; on better understanding their geopolitical, cultural, and biological roots; and on formulating the multilateral, multi-sector, collaborative, and innovative solutions necessary to address these problems on both the local and global level.

I have heard the authors refer to this as a situation where "practice is leading theory," which to my mind means that if you can clear away the fog surrounding the issue, there is a big idea underneath. And this big idea has significant implications for all of us. The megacommunity idea will lead us to the sorts of solutions that can effectively address complex issues—and not a moment too soon.

Walter Isaacson
President and CEO of the Aspen Institute

PREFACE

We began to work on this book, though we didn't fully realize it at the time, in an executive summit meeting that we hosted in December 2002 for our firm, Booz Allen Hamilton. A little more than one year before, the World Trade Center towers collapsed and a terrorist-controlled plane crashed into the U.S. Pentagon. The government of the United States was now considering a preemptive invasion of Iraq, in the hopes of preventing a more destructive future attack. This series of events was leading to palpable disorientation and uncertainty. We were also keenly aware of other uncertainties facing business leaders and the world in general.

Some of our colleagues at Booz Allen Hamilton had worked on developing plans for preventing or responding to new pandemic diseases, such as the HN51 virus, or "Avian flu," which, beginning with the 1997 outbreak in Hong Kong, was becoming increasingly associated with human deaths. Other colleagues were working closely with organizations trying to deal with the problems of an interconnected global economic sphere: companies trying to outsource their production and innovation methods, national and local governments seeking to hold onto jobs and autonomy, and a growing number of "non-governmental organizations" (or "civil society" groups) who were trying to fill the gaps in social welfare and protection left by the other two sectors.

Against this backdrop of increasing uncertainty, 22 chief executive officers from some of the largest and most influential companies in the world came together at Booz Allen's summit, prepared to discuss the greatest challenges facing businesses today. They focused on the need to manage risk and control disruptions in the new operating environment and to create resilience in their enterprises.

As we started talking, we realized that none of the corporate leaders in the room felt like they had the answer to the questions most on their minds: "How can we keep our businesses, and the communities in which we operate, reasonably safe? Indeed, how can we continue to create strong, extended enterprises in a world of ever more complicated problems and crises?" They were looking for answers within their organizations, and not finding many. Some of them had begun to extend this search well beyond the walls of their companies. In the end, the summit attendees concluded that three things would have to happen for a reliable answer to emerge:

- Public–private partnerships should be redefined to align with the new operating reality.
- New types of market incentives should appear to address long-term resilience.

• Leaders of business and government around the world should design new economic mitigation strategies that avoid market spikes due to crisis decisions.

We also came away from the summit discussions convinced that there was both interest in, and an urgent need for, some new ways of thinking that could offer leaders the tools they needed for better focus, investment effectiveness, accountability, and global partnerships.

Over the next two years, Booz Allen Hamilton conducted several strategic simulations in which stakeholders play out fabricated crises. Although they addressed different issues—HIV/AIDS in India, port security, and bioterrorism—we found we could draw a similar lesson from each.

In the bioterrorism simulation, for example, we saw the real need for industry and government to collaborate on the knowledge and distribution of key medicines where decision velocity was the key to reducing mortality. In the port security simulation, we discovered the importance of public- and private-sector collaboration to ensure the integrity of our ports without disrupting our economic trade. In the HIV/AIDS simulation, we saw powerful evidence of the need for a coordinated public–private approach to this health crisis, spurring new partnerships and initiatives to fight the epidemic. In other words, all of these simulations indicated the need for a new type of tri-sector mechanism and mindset.

Then in March 2005, we jointly hosted another highly cooperative experience in China. This event—addressing HIV/AIDS in China—

brought together more than 300 leaders from local Chinese and multinational corporations active in China. The event confirmed the validity of our hypothesis that the critical global issues facing us today are mutual concerns which can only be addressed in a shared manner. Any approach to addressing them must have value for all stakeholders: government, business, and civil society.

Our involvement in these simulations represented life-changing turning points for the authors of this book. We recognized that the combination of our understanding and experience in building government/business/NGO practices put us in a unique position to address some of the burgeoning problems among all three sectors.

Booz Allen started to question and challenge itself in terms of our view on globalization, what its practical implications were, and, most importantly, what we would advise our clients to do differently: solutions for tomorrow. We examined all of the literature on globalization. While it was interesting and instructive, we were surprised that it very seldom addressed what's next, or provided an action plan.

We had witnessed how, with the proper plan in place, even a major "shared leadership deficit"—where inherent, seemingly unresolvable tensions exist among stakeholders—can be transformed into a satisfying relationship and highly effective solutions. What is required are leaders who know how to identify the vital interests they share with others, who are prepared to seek the benefits from which all can gain, and who are committed to addressing these issues. We also saw how easy this philosophy was to espouse, and how difficult it was to actually put into practice. But, during the various simulations, we had experienced firsthand that it *can* be put into practice. Deliberate and informed actions *can* turn around systems of tension. They *can* draw out a kind of dynamic balance, an equilibrium grounded in both better communication and better cross-organizational structures. And this equilibrium, in turn, *can* serve as a basis for a sustaining partnership with leaders in the other sectors.

But while we felt we understood the value of this new type of deliberate equilibrium, and while we had seen it in operation, we weren't quite sure how to articulate the critical differences that would allow people to put it reliably into practice. So we decided to seek some wisdom from the outside. Over the next six months, we conducted extensive interviews with more than 100 leaders from the public, private, and civil society sectors. This book came to life through these conversations. In fact, quotes from these interviews are dispersed throughout our book. While not all interviewees are quoted directly, each contributed significantly to our understanding of the issues, options, and barriers associated with megacommunities.

The extensive list of participants came from all regions of the world—the United States, Canada, Europe, Latin America, Africa, Australia, and Asia. They included such formidable political figures as Bill Clinton, Henry Kissinger, Singapore's Minister of Foreign Affairs George Yong-Boon Yeo, and former Spanish Prime Minister José María Aznar. We also engaged such business luminaries as CEO Richard Parsons of Time Warner, Kenneth Chenault of American Express, former CEO of Hong Kong Telecom Linus Cheung, and Fulvio Conti, CEO of Enel SpA in Italy. Our wide-ranging roster includes educators, strategists, advertising executives, several ambassadors, and numerous heads of leading NGOs. We tapped into organizations as diverse as the European Space Agency, YouthAIDS, Young & Rubicam, Peking University, Harvard University, the U.S. State Department, Audi, and the International Campaign to Ban Landmines.

These interviews confirmed our growing suspicion: Leaders were looking for both new techniques to help solve complex problems and they were looking for a broad-based perspective that would allow them to create successful partnerships in a global economy. Our interviews covered the growing need for fluid, multi-sector interactions that will help leaders reconcile benefits and inequities—sooner, rather than later in the heat of conflict.

It took another two years of synthesis, experimentation, and observation, working with colleagues and clients around the world, to draw our themes together. During that time, the value of the tri-sector approach became more and more evident to us, and we believe it has also become evident to others. Out of this need for an effective tri-sector approach, we developed our concept of "megacommunity"–an idea that will help leaders cope with the challenges created by the *global dynamics* environment, in part by transcending some traditional ways of thinking that have blocked solutions in the past. The concept of megacommunity draws heavily on the fields of network theory, group dynamics, and behavioral economics, but always in the service of the goal of sustained solutions to problems that no single organization (or methodology) can solve alone.

We conceived of this book as a way to not just describe the megacommunity concept, but to help leaders better understand the global dynamic challenges they face, and develop the new skills necessary to address these challenges. Through our experience with diverse clients in various settings over the past decade, we have come to see how difficult it can be for leaders to embrace the decentralized and networked reality within which they operate. We recognize that this is a situation where practice is leading theory. Hence, it is our intention to address the need by describing, in concrete and understandable terms, the theory behind the practice of building megacommunities so that it can be both replicated at scale and improved through examination.

We acknowledge that not every megacommunity needs to engage in every suggestion made in the book. In the development of megacommunities, it is important to drive the theory to the surface, so to speak, in order to unlock and unpack the megacommunity concept as thoroughly as possible. And it is equally important to define a primary set of actions. Any megacommunity will be stronger for considering the strategies found here.

We would like to emphasize at the outset that this is not another book that simply "admires the problem," or one that offers yet another framework to capture the essence of the problem. This book is first, and foremost, a guide for leaders—a book that provides a definitive course of action. Because our discussion by necessity covers so much ground—value chain analysis, system dynamics, and behavioral economics—we have provided a simple glossary to help navigate some of the terms we use in the megacommunity arena that may not be familiar to you.

Our book develops a practical model of collective leadership called the megacommunity in which no one leader or institution is necessarily in charge, and yet a healthy, prosperous, effectual environment exists in which issues are addressed and complexity is reduced. In the chapters that follow, you will find a practical program that leaders can put into action immediately.

We are not positing the idea that the megacommunity supplants all other forms of networked governance, multilateral engagements, or partnerships. Our client experience shows quite clearly that there are, and will continue to be, requirements that are met quite well by these engagement forums. But there is a gap. We have all experienced a distinct set of issues—usually distinguishable by their complexity—that are not solvable by these well-established means.

This book aims to close that gap.

MEGACOMMUNITIES

CHAPTER ONE

AN INTERDEPENDENT WORLD IN CRISIS

One of the most powerful hurricanes to ever strike the United States—not just in its physical impact, but its influence on human affairs—was Hurricane Andrew. The hurricane's 165-mile-an-hour winds slammed into Florida's Atlantic coast, scattering trees and cars, turning businesses and homes into shattered piles of debris, and rapidly overwhelming local relief efforts. One of the most visible community leaders, Dade County Emergency Management Director Kate Hale, appeared on national television blaming the federal government, who in her mind was supposed to ride to the rescue. "Where in the hell is the cavalry on this one?" she asked. "They keep saying we're going to get supplies. For God's sake, where are they?"

That's the natural response to so many of the complex problems we face these days, whether it's a terrorist attack, an economic crisis, a looming health pandemic, a gradual decline in some important indicator of economic or social health, or the anxieties unleashed by the forces of globalization. We always expect the cavalry to ride in, to save the day like they would in an archetypal Western movie. Thirteen years after Andrew struck, the citizens and civic leaders of New Orleans implicitly asked the same question about the 2005 Hurricane Katrina disaster: Who was expected to take charge of, first, preventing the floods and, second, rescuing people from them?

Many felt that the Federal Emergency Management Agency (FEMA) failed to respond effectively to Hurricane Katrina. But despite FEMA's perceived failings, it's a mistake to think that any single agency could completely fulfill the required roles. Indeed, for any complex situation anywhere in the world, it's become obvious that there is no one authority—whether in the form of a leader, an organization, a command operation, or a rescue squad—that can single-handedly save the day. Some other kind of leadership is needed.

And what form might that take? One place to find an answer is in the aftermath of Hurricane Andrew. The hurricane served, as then-Florida Governor Jeb Bush later put it, as a wake-up call for everyone in the state. A relevant article[1] by our colleagues Doug Himberger, Dave Sulek, and Stephan Krill of Booz Allen Hamilton described the resulting impact this way:

Ultimately, Andrew destroyed 126,000 homes, left 250,000 people homeless, wiped out 80 percent of the area's farms, and was responsible for at least 40 deaths. The hurricane also caused more than $26 billion in damage, including $16 billion in insured losses—too much for insurance companies to cover. According to one report, 11 insurance companies went bankrupt trying to cover more than 600,000 claims.

Specifically, it was now clear to Florida's leaders that no government agency could manage this type of large-scale catastrophe on its own. . . . So Florida moved to a new approach, deliberately involving a variety of organizations—public sector, corporate, nongovernmental (NGOs), and faith-based—in its emergency planning and activities. This meant changing both the planning process and the relationships among these various groups.

The success of this approach soon became obvious. During the severe 2004 and 2005 hurricane seasons, a series of high-powered hurricanes and tropical storms (Hurricanes Charley, Frances, Ivan, Jeanne, Dennis, Katrina, Rita, and Wilma, and Tropical Storms Bonnie, Ophelia, and Tammy) struck Florida. The state's government, business, and civil organizations quickly mobilized, working together—as they had planned and trained to do—to provide aid for relief and recovery. At the same time, strengthened building codes limited the damage to businesses and homes. Following the 2004 hurricane season, insurance companies received more than $3.6 billion from [a new] catastrophe fund, cushioning the impact of claims they paid for storm damages. Florida still requested federal assistance during these crises, reinforcing the federal government's critical role in assisting during response and recovery. But the federal government was just one of many members of an integrated [group of organizations, each with] its own particular role and purpose. Consequently, when hurricanes threaten Florida today, its residents no longer expect or require the federal "cavalry" to sweep in and save the day.

This new model for collective leadership stands in stark contrast to the efforts following Hurricane Katrina. And indeed, Florida played an integral role in supporting southern Mississippi and Louisiana during Katrina's aftermath. Within hours of the storm's landfall, Florida began deploying more than 3,700 first responders to the affected areas.

The most important principle to draw from examples like Katrina and Andrew is the need for a new approach to tackling these complex issues, supported by a new model of leadership. Fortunately, such a model is emerging. And where it has taken root, it has had immensely beneficial and dramatic effects. The purpose of this book is to explain the model, show how it can be effective, and give leaders around the world—and citizens and participants—the conceptual tools and examples they need to put it into practice.

The name we give to this model is the "megacommunity"—a name based on the idea that communities of organizations, as vehicles for large-scale change, are both feasible and needed as they never have been before. Megacommunities are not large communities of people; they are communities of organizations whose leaders and members have deliberately come together across national, organizational, and sectoral boundaries to reach the goals they cannot achieve alone. The action planning embedded in a megacommunity goes far beyond many well-meaning (but incomplete) ideas about the social role of business, such as corporate social responsibility, triple bottom-line reporting, or sustainable development. The scope of a megacommunity exceeds that of public–private partnerships that tend toward limited alliances over relatively short-term periods, and typically focus on relatively narrow purposes. Megacommunities take on much larger goals that are ongoing and mutable over time. Most importantly, *megacommunities demand a change in orientation from the leaders of the various organizations involved.*

FRAMING THE PROBLEM

Before we begin to outline the megacommunity approach in detail, it's necessary to take a closer look at what drives the situation in which we find ourselves. We need to explore the texture, nature, and sources of these new multi-layered challenges. After all, Hurricane Katrina is only one (albeit still-raw) example of the kind of the elaborate problems we currently face. Large-scale challenges of unprecedented complexity—related to global and national security, economic well-being, and the health and safety of citizens around the world—have increasingly become critical issues for leaders of governments, businesses, and civil society institutions. Some of these issues have high global public profiles, such as climate change, cyber security, preparing for pandemics, and terrorism. Others, such as water scarcity, aging populations, obsolete urban infrastructure, and sustainable energy, are important, but more distant issues. But all are poised to become massive public and private challenges in the next few years. We say "massive" because of certain critical common traits that each of these issues share.

First, these issues exhibit a high degree of interconnectedness and interdependence: They affect people outside the narrow boundaries of a nation-state or an industry. Energy policy in Russia affects natural gas prices throughout Europe; environmental decisions in rural Italy can have a dramatic effect on energy choices elsewhere in Europe.

Second, the complex interactions that define these issues also compound the impact. Surrounding these issues are non-linear forms of activity in which such factors as capital flow, demographics, technology dispersion, energy supply, and emissions gradually accelerate, until they cross a "tipping point" and are experienced as sudden, dramatic shifts in quality of life.

Third, these events abruptly and unpredictably escalate, outpacing our ability to respond. By the time a corporation notices that its customers have perceived a drop in quality; or a city's water system bursts at rush hour; or a pension system becomes manifestly incapable of fulfilling its promises to citizens, it may well be too late to do much about it.

Each of these problems comes with its own set of specific cascading effects, but they've also had a generalized negative effect on leadership. These problems often seem intractable because solutions in the past have backfired or gone awry. As a result, in recent years, galloping frustration and confusion has led to a stultifying crisis in confidence. Leaders everywhere no longer discuss the future with as much exhilaration as they once did. When speaking candidly, they often sound as if they are trapped in quicksand, unable to move forward easily. The methods and tools that helped them succeed in the past no longer work.

Across all three power sectors—business, the government, and civil society—fresh solutions are desperately needed. In multinational corporations, "everybody is frozen," as American Express Chairman and CEO Kenneth Chenault expressed in our discussions with him. More than ever, the ability to seize opportunities or make a profit depends on unfamiliar and unpredictable factors, such as the reputation of the company's supply chain partners, the stability of local governments in distant countries, and a grasp of changing global trends. But, according to Chenault, a fundamental level of insight is missing. "What has not kept pace in the business world," he says, "is an understanding of how the uncertainty of the geopolitical environment has impacted business."

Governments, meanwhile, have reached something akin to an identity crisis following 20-plus years of economic bonanza in which businesses have had the upper hand. They struggle to play their fundamental role, that of managing the problems of public society. In a world of constant changes and rising pressures, many governments seem unarmed and incapable of intermediating between mercantile phenomena and the common good, and can no longer spend or regulate their way into requisite solutions. "In the past, corporations could depend on the fact that government defined the answers," says Stephen Merrill, formerly the governor of New Hampshire and currently president of Bingham Consulting Group LLC. But now, he says, business leaders are afraid that "government doesn't even understand the questions."

For their part, civil society players are also experiencing a confounding sea change. Civil society, also known as the "non-profit world" and the "third sector," is distinct from government and business. It represents a collection of so-called nongovernmental organizations (NGOs) and intermediary institutions such as professional associations, religious groups, labor unions, and citizen advocacy organizations. The civil society sector gives voice to various groups and eases public participation in decision processes. Although expanding communications and the Internet have given these organizations more of a global voice than ever before, the demand for their work has increased commensurately, competition for funding has escalated, and they no longer understand constituents' needs as easily as they used to. "We've had blinders on," says Paul Leonard, former CEO of Habitat for Humanity International. "We need to change course, to become more of a partner and a player; more knowledgeable about the large systems that exist and the role we can play in them."

In essence, and simply, what's affecting most leaders is the fact that problems have reached an enormously new level of complexity. And this new complexity manifests itself on every level, from the local/regional (as in the case of Katrina) to the global—where we leap directly into the mire known as "*geocomplexity.*"

In fact, the realm of geocomplexity is the best place to begin our journey toward the need for megacommunity. The kinds of problems that a megacommunity can solve are most starkly revealed around issues of geocomplexity—in particular, around the issue of "sustainable globalization." As we'll see, there is an imperative behind sustainable globalization that makes the conditions ripe for a new approach, which makes the need for megacommunity solutions crucial.

SUSTAINABLE GLOBALIZATION

As Driss Jettou, prime minister of Morocco points out, "there is no one definition of globalization." For the purposes of this book, when using "globalization," we are referring to the increasing interdependence of human activity and trading relationships around the world, enabled by new forms of technology and communications, and by new types of financial connections.

Too often, the media and many policy makers view the current wave of globalization as a totally unprecedented phenomenon in economic history. But as George Yong-Boon Yeo, Singapore's minister of Foreign Affairs, sharply expressed in our talks with him, "Globalization is not new. It's always been part of the cyclical change in human affairs." Since the first humans migrated out of Africa, communities have struggled to balance their need for autonomy against the benefits and risks of contact with others. Great conquering civilizations—the Egyptian, the Greek, the Roman, the Spanish, the British—each established a system of trade for goods, and every one of these systems collapsed as the single empire behind them became stretched too thin, or collided with a stronger military force. Those deep fluctuations continued into modern history. Historians agree, for example, that there was an immense wave of globalization at the end of the nineteenth century, when continental railroads and steamships were made possible by the invention of steel, and when the telegraph, the undersea cable, and the first waves of electromagnetic energy expanded the reach of communications dramatically. This wave came to an end, arguably, with the beginning of World

War I and was not relaunched in earnest until after World War II, with the Marshall Plan and the Bretton Woods agreements.

Since then, globalization has been fueled by another wave, that of technology—computers, the Internet, air transportation, logistics innovation, and biotechnology—all of which continues to unfold. This technology boom has resulted in the biggest economic stimulus in history, given the fact that the industrial revolution involved only one-third of the world's population at the time, while the current tech revolution involves a larger percentage of the world's current population of six billion. Moreover, technology allows us to move at a speed that can, in a short time frame, unleash a sudden, violent burst of economic activity in a certain country and/or geographical area, often followed by an equally violent withdrawal of that activity. Such scale and rapidity are unprecedented in history.

Today, flows of people, money, information, and goods around the world are more distributed, more networked, and seemingly random, with dynamic changes occurring at unprecedented speed. Global reach and influence have hit levels undreamed of 20 years ago. And it is important to remember that we are not seeing only a growing number of linkages, but a growing *density* of linkages among people, organizations, and issues all across the world. For the first time in human history, the number of people living in cities is larger than the number living in rural areas, and the migration from rural to urban is, if anything, accelerating.

While the density of these linkages increases complexity, they afford us incredible advantages—faster decisions, quicker access to information, and an extended set of potential capabilities (that is, new abilities, methods, and tools). The current globalization cycle has also led to profound structural changes: the development of overlapping social networks (such as the professional associations by which business leaders, regulators, and medical professionals seek each others' advice), new rules of law (such as the international treaties governing intellectual property and responses to climate change), and new governance structures (the European Union, North American Free Trade Association, the African Union, the Pacific Islands Forum, and so on). The entire economies of certain countries—particularly developing ones—are based on their ability to participate in the system. India is perhaps the best example of this, with its central role in outsourcing and its technical service industry driving its economic growth. Since 1985, the number of Indians defined as "deprived" has fallen from 93 percent to 54 percent of the population, as 103 million people moved out of desperate poverty and many millions more were born into less dire circumstances.

But as with many things in life, these accelerated changes can also lead to great uncertainties. While economic growth makes developing countries better off on the whole, not everyone is a winner. The increase of economic growth around the planet is already straining the availability of water, energy, and other natural resources. It has accelerated the carbon emissions that are, almost certainly, contributing significantly to climate change. And the ability to reach out across national and organizational boundaries, to exchange information, financing, and weaponry, is one of the critical elements in the arsenal of present-day terrorists. Finally, and perhaps most importantly, exposure to every type of incoming influence—from microscopic biological predators to undocumented workers—has the ability to reach more deeply into local communities with potentially long term effects.

With so many profound changes happening at such a rapid rate, and with the unintended consequences that have emerged from the "Washington consensus"[2] and many other efforts to set new standards for economic practice, some opposition to globalization should have been expected. It should also have been expected that the sporadic violent opposition of the late 1990s and early 2000s would subside into more persistent, but less energetic, "globalization fatigue." The backlash against globalization manifests itself these days in new trade barriers and protectionist policies (e.g., the United States, Europe, and China have both signaled such a path in recent years on agricultural and textile issues) and in "anti-globalization" meetings such as the World Social Forum. The sacking of the European Union constitution by France and Holland in 2005 epitomizes the general fear of global melding in the public sector, further stoked by mounting resentment of job loss due to off-shoring and outsourcing.

This type of backsliding occurred at least once before in modern history, between 1904 and 1914, in the decade preceding World War I. Like today, that period was marked by great-power rivalry, unstable alliances, rogue regimes, and terrorist organizations. And the world is no better prepared for calamity now. Paolo Scaroni, CEO of ENI, the leading integrated oil company in Italy, and former CEO of the Italian energy company ENEL SpA, warns that indeed, "Globalization can go back. It did in the past and it might in the future." In a worst-case scenario, the devolution of globalization could mean that the future of humanity will be one of further fragmentation, sectarianism, economic malaise, insularity, and possibly greater war.

What's needed, in short, is a form of sustainable globalization that provides net benefits through expanded opportunity without short-changing the viability of local life. The word "sustainable" in this context dates back to 1983, when the United Nations Brundtland Commission (chaired by then-President of Norway Gro Harlem Brundtland) defined sustainable development as development that "meets the needs of the present without compromising the ability of future generations to meet their own needs."[3]

Leaders from all ends of the political spectrum need to develop the tools to make globalization sustainable. Until we reach some common understanding of how to deal with sustainable globalization, we will not be able to find a reasonable balance, in most communities, between economic growth (the expansion of opportunities) and equity (the welfare of the entire community).

THREE LIMITING FACTORS

To be sure, sustainable globalization—as we've described it—is not an easy goal to achieve. It would mean simultaneously overcoming three ingrained limits:

1) THE LIMITS OF HUMAN CAPACITY FOR UNDERSTANDING COMPLEXITY ITSELF

As cultural critic Fredric Jameson notes, the challenges inherent in contact with so many outside forces are so vast and diverse that they have moved beyond the "categories of perception with which human beings normally orient themselves."[4] It is the difficulty of grasping the complexity of our global structures that triggers so much visceral anxiety and insecurity on the part of leaders everywhere.

One of the major reasons for this disorientation is the lack of a definable epicenter—a problem that earlier episodes of globalization did not seem to face. In the nineteenth century, for example, Britain served as the axis for global expansion, a center so solid that politician Lord Salisbury popularly remarked that it was an empire on which "the sun never sets."[5] The currently globalized world does not have a clear, definitive locus that generates such confidence; a few years ago, one might have heard comments that we are entering an "American century," but economic and military dominance no longer seems preordained for the United States. Emerging countries are becoming ever more prominent; their share of world exports has jumped from 20 percent in 1970 to 40 percent today. These countries consume half of the world's energy, account for four-fifths of the growth in oil demand, and hold 70 percent of world's exchange reserves. This means that rich countries no longer dominate the world economy. In fact, as British historian Niall Ferguson remarks in his book *The War of the World—History's Age of Hatred,*[6] the zenith of the Western world power belongs to the past.

Another key factor limiting human capacity for understanding global complexity is the complete lack of predictability inherent in this new wave of globalization. We like to know—or at least have a feel for—what will happen under a given set of conditions. The unfortunate truth is that the interconnectedness and interdependence associated with sustainable globalization creates a dynamic environment in which even small actions have big, unexpected consequences. Think also of your own experience—how easy is it to predict the outcome of your decisions? How often do you uncover unintended consequences in what seemed like the best course of action? Network theorists give this phenomenon a poetic name—the "butterfly effect" (that is, the notion that a butterfly flapping its wings in Africa can set in motion a chain of events that can result in a hurricane that hits the coast of Florida). Poetic names and descriptors aside, real world examples abound: a rogue trader in Singapore brings down a global investment firm single-handedly; a shoe manufacturer is brought to its knees by an NGO drawing attention to its labor practices in Indonesia. The ultimate victim of the butterfly effect is confidence in linear, cause-and-effect predictability. Whether running a business or playing chess, human beings draw comfort from being able to predict the consequences of a certain set of actions. That comfort level has all but disappeared in our current global environment.

2) THE RARITY OF GENUINE DIALOGUE ON WHAT GLOBALIZATION REALLY MEANS

Another limiting factor that needs to be overcome is the meaning of "globalization." Since the term first surfaced in the 1960s, it has been used as an excuse to blame opponents for perceived problems as diverse as labor costs, environmental regulation, and the dominance of an undemocratic "new world order." Globalization has proven to be a surprisingly subjective concept, and many people find themselves unable to talk about either its nature or their own goals.

For example, for many in the business community, globalization basically remains the process by which a company enters the domain of international commerce. Dick Parsons, CEO of Time Warner, defines the typical business attitude on globalization as a journey through four practical phases. First, a business leader begins exporting products that were once created for a domestic market. Then, the business creates a global distribution and marketing infrastructure while continuing to make products at home. Then, the business starts to manufacture and design products outside the home market for non-domestic markets. Finally, the business creates products anywhere in the world, exporting them directly to other markets, including back to the country of origin.

By contrast, some leaders focus on the loftier dimension of cross-boundary communication. Singapore's Minister of Foreign Affairs George Yong-Boon Yeo likens the growth of global openness to the development of an IT protocol. Just as networked computers can communicate, despite running on different operating systems, globalization serves as a "higher order language" enabling the countries of the world to communicate in spite of their cultural differences.

Other political leaders are more interested in the problems of mutual support. "Globalization means the concept of global village," says Kaifu Luo, chairman and president of China National Foreign Trade Transportation Group. Reflecting on the rapid pace of China's economic growth, Luo underscores the importance of inclusiveness and a shared development agenda. "Globalization is saying your development cannot be separate from mine," he states, "and my development should not be—and cannot be—separate from yours. We should be walking together."

Similarly, M. K. Bhan, secretary to the government of India, Department of Biotechnology, discusses globalization in the context of the importance of partnerships on an international scale. "To me, what globalization really means is that in terms of proper development, trade, and innovation, we do not think of partnerships within the country, but you think of them on a global scale, which means joint discovery, joint partnerships and innovation, partnerships in trade, partnerships in technology."

Others talk about overcoming the imbalance among "haves" and "have-nots"—within or among countries. Economist Hernando De Soto, for example, views globalization in the context of its ability to address unequal participation in the global economy. By his estimate, "Four billion people across the world are locked out of globalization because they have no formal property rights, and therefore occupy the extralegal sector. . . . We need to make the only thing that seems to bring great prosperity—the market system—work."

Former European Union Competition Commissioner Mario Monti agrees. "Globalization is sustainable in the long period only if it is somehow also a balanced process and in particular if it allows for the development of a consensus even of the 'losers' of the globalization process."

We have found that some leaders instinctively seek solutions that are participative and inclusive, grounded in the "wisdom of crowds," abetted by telecommunications links that bring together opinions from around the globe. Others are horrified by this cacophony, this rule of the mob. They are like the World Economic Forum's Jean-François Rischard, who recently proposed that global problems should be solved by recruiting top experts in each of 20 arenas, and literally shipping them off in groups to isolated islands for several years until they return with solutions. Still others, disheartened by the track record of experts, prefer the accountability of elected officials; while others, perceiving elected officials as swamped by bureaucracy and beholden to special interests, argue that entrepreneurs are the only leaders who can solve problems. Each of these approaches, in its own way, represents its own effort to "shift the burden" of finding a solution onto some other group—whether it's the crowd, the expert, the authority, or the entrepreneur, let it be someone other than ourselves who has to find a solution.

One thing is clear: Until we have a genuine dialogue on these core issues, any solution we come up with will be partial at best and inadequate to address the challenge.

3) EACH SECTOR HAS SEPARATE TRADITIONS FOR DEALING WITH GLOBALIZATION, AND THEY HAVE NOT LEARNED TO TRANSCEND THOSE HABITUAL BARRIERS

It's easy to accept the proposition that every individual business leader, policymaker, or NGO director has a vision of how to capitalize on the global operating environment. But these visions, as well as the associated strategies for achieving objectives, are too often designed from a single-sector point of view. They are not aligned with the overall globalized system within which they must operate. Yet globalization has made the three sectors so interdependent, isolation is not an option. Thus, the ability to execute a global strategy over the long term by effectively and continually managing the dynamic interfaces between all three sectors has become a critical skill, all too often unrecognized by government, business, or the civil sector—especially those agencies, companies, and organizations that fail.

Perhaps the leaders of the three sectors could overcome their differences if there were enough effective venues and forums within which they could meet and talk candidly. According to John Ruggie, Director of the Center for Business and Government at Harvard University's Kennedy School of Government (and currently the UN's Special Representative on the Issue of Human Rights and Transnational Corporations and Other Business Enterprises), "There is no 'collective action' body at the international level to balance the system. The World Economic Forum might be the closest, but it is more about talk than action." He adds, "The UN Global Compact is an example of a 'strategic entry point' for dialogue, but not a force in and of itself to help to balance the sectors."

Meanwhile, world institutions such as the United Nations, the International Monetary Fund, and the World Bank may be discussing needed reforms but, so far, they are not agreeing on much. (In some ways, these bodies—all constituted in the 1940s—might be seen as holdovers from a different era with an outmoded sense of mission.) Clearly, a new type of entry point for collective action is needed, one that is available to all the stakeholders, local and global.

Lodewijk Christiaan van Wachem, former chairman of the supervisory board of the Royal Dutch Petroleum Company, a position he held through July 2002, sees globalization, in its essence, "as a mindset." And he is right. Globalization, at its core, is a new mindset, a new consciousness that has already taken hold. If we want to make this mindset sustainable, then it needs some profound—but very feasible—adjustments.

THE IMPORTANCE OF BUILDING NETWORK CAPITAL

Imagine if we could overcome those limits just discussed, and find a pathway not only to sustainable globalization, but to sustainability in all our efforts. The benefits, both direct and indirect, would be enormous. As Elio Catania, former chairman and CEO of Italian Railways, states, "The more sustainable a strategy is, the more spontaneously results arrive." In the past two decades, globalization has brought increased returns on investments and regional stability, as well as expanding access to food, water, shelter, clothes and education, among other resources. "If one wants to eradicate poverty, or deal with AIDS," says Kenneth Chenault, "there are now a set of platforms and processes where the best-practice sharing can be accelerated. You can bring resources from a wide variety of sources geographically."

The findings of the 2003 World Trade Organization report showed that less globalized countries saw per capita income growth of 0.9 percent per year, while those countries that were highly globalized saw per capita incomes grow by 4.3 percent annually.[9] India, for example, is lifting itself out of poverty on the rising tide of globalization. China has adopted solid structural economic reforms that are beginning to pay off solidly and is seeing the number of citizens living in poverty decline. The countries of the former Soviet Union—including Russia itself—are developing into stable economic players on this wave.

Businesses, meanwhile, have adapted and built into their models the knowledge of markets and technology that are the attributes of today's global economy. Large and small businesses alike have grown dependent on these models. The most vivid demonstration of this concept is the explosive growth of global supply chains. It is not difficult to imagine what would happen to the world economy if there were a major series of breaches in this flow of goods, services, and capital. For example, a port security wargame conducted by Booz Allen in 2002 showed that a 14-day port closure would result in a $56 billion hit to the U.S. economy.[8] And consider what kind of cultural disruptions would occur if economic globalization proves unsustainable while the "soft globalization" of Internet-driven ideas and opinions rapidly advances.

What, then, is an effective strategy for maintaining sustainable globalization? A government's sustainability may be based on the maintenance of political capital. Civil society's vision of sustainability may focus on the social capital necessary for channels in which various groups and individuals can actively participate in critical decision-making processes. A company's economic sustainability may be based on the maintenance of financial capital.

But as former President Bill Clinton points out, "Globalization to me is much more than an economic concept. It's about the increasing interdependence of people in the world. . . . It's very difficult to have a global financial system and a global economic system when you don't have the global political or social system."

So, we believe, the essential basis for sustainable globalization—and sustainability in general—is the maintenance of *network capital*. Globalization strategies often stretch across sectors and wide geographic areas. As the number and density of such connections grows, so do the challenges of relationship management. Gone are the days when leaders could predictably manage their strategies as a closed system with easily identifiable starting and ending points. The global economy is taking on the properties of an extremely complex network. Networks, by their very nature, involve distributing direct control over significant operations throughout the network, and substituting negotiated relationships for hierarchical structures.

What we need is a new mechanism to build network capital. This new mechanism would have several features. It would bring people together—by which we mean enabling people to recognize their common ground and goals. It would involve all three sectors—government, business, and the civil sector—with no one of them dominating. And it would use self-reinforcing activities—what psychologist Ellen Langer calls "the power of mindful thinking"—to reduce overwhelming complexity.

It would also be approachable, accessible by any organization of any size confronting this new complexity—from a village group trying to decide how to market its crafts to a local business to a regional authority to the European Union and the United Nations. This mechanism would have to be competent and effective enough to draw in a variety of people—those who are afraid of the "rule of the mob," those who want experts or large groups to save us, and those who distrust authority figures. The mechanism needs to be useful in local as well as global settings; it needs to recognize the ways in which local and global perspectives influence each other, and it needs to offer a set of solutions that can scale up and down as necessary.

In the following chapters, we will define and illustrate how to use this new mechanism, which we call "megacommunity." In many ways, our current economic reality is beginning to self-select this mechanism because it holds out the hope of performing most effectively in the long run, and because capital loves moving to the superior performers in a system. Society is also selecting this mechanism because people love a venue in which they can solve problems openly and effectively. That, in fact, is the very nature of the megacommunity.

CHAPTER TWO

ANATOMY OF A MEGACOMMUNITY

What, then, is a megacommunity made of? Probably the best way to begin answering this question is through one of the many scenarios we've encountered that led us directly—and inexorably—to the megacommunity concept.

Consider the upheaval that occurred in the Italian city of Brindisi when a new regasifying terminal was proposed in the early 2000s. Enel SpA, Italy's leading utility provider, had been seeking to diversify its sources of natural gas. It joined forces with the UK company British Gas (BG). Together they planned to build a terminal for regasifying liquefied natural gas in Brindisi, an economically depressed area situated on the heel of Italy's proverbial boot.

The company expected their project to be greeted with popular support. After all, their plans involved the search for new, cleaner sources of energy, a good thing by any standard. And the project would have provided 1,000 jobs during its three years of planned construction and 250 permanent new jobs in the region.

Enel SpA and BG were very careful to fulfill all the legal requirements necessary for starting the project, making sure their lawyers were involved from the beginning, as most companies do when facing a potentially controversial project or a project with local political ramifications. But their legal outreach turned out to be far from sufficient to offset what quickly became a long and unprofitable chain of events. Soon after the project began, environmental activists published a paper highlighting its danger to the environment and the beauty of Brindisi's coast. The paper triggered a much larger protest, amplified by the local press into a broad and persistent national issue. In October 2003, a civil petition with more than 10,000 signatures brought the first official halt to the project. In July 2005, more than 8,000 protesters took to the streets, shouting, "We must save Brindisi!" A few weeks later, construction was entirely shut down. Although Italy's Supreme Court stepped in and construction began again four months later, Enel SpA ultimately felt the need to withdraw from the venture, selling its 50 percent investment back to BG.

Although this project has not yet concluded at the time of this writing and BG still hopes to build the terminal, the outcome created a series of radiating effects. It left Enel SpA heavily dependent on Russian and North African natural gas pipelines, which, in turn, rely on cartels for their supply. In addition, the two companies are less cost competitive since the start of the venture, thus the shareholders get lower returns. Enel's customers pay higher prices for natural gas. And the 250 new jobs projected for Brindisi are nowhere to be seen.

Surely, there are things Enel SpA and BG could have done differently. In many ways, they were treated as an incursive force because they acted like one. They should not have allowed themselves to believe that clearing legal hurdles was enough. They should have been aware that their project involved a wider array of stakeholders. They should have engaged the public directly. And working together with the government and civil society, they should have developed a heightened awareness of intersecting goals, both local and global. In other words, like so many companies, governments, and NGOs that make similar mistakes, Enel SpA could and should have initiated a megacommunity.

As we discussed in chapter one, a megacommunity is a public sphere in which organizations from three sectors—business, government, and civil society—deliberately join together around compelling issues of mutual importance, following a set of practices and principles that make it easier for them to achieve results without sacrificing their individual goals. We chose the term megacommunity to reflect such a sphere's character as a gathering place, not of individuals, but of organizations.

Like a business environment, a megacommunity contains organizations that sometimes compete and sometimes collaborate. But a megacommunity is not strictly a business niche. The story of Enel in

Brindisi—that is, the story of a non-local business entering a new environment—represents only one potential starting point for megacommunity. We've observed megacommunity-like phenomena occurring around issues as diverse as preserving old-growth forests, healthcare in Rhode Island, "fair trade" coffee, small-business survival, even the management of such shared resources as the lands of Antarctica and the Great Barrier Reef. A megacommunity is any large ongoing sphere of interest where governments, corporations, NGOs, and others intersect over time. The participants remain interdependent because their common interest compels them to work together, even though they might not see, describe, or approach their mutual problem or situation in the same way.

While the megacommunity concept calls on all of these sectors to interact according to their common interests, it does not call on them to compromise their unique priorities. And it certainly does not call on them to eschew their responsibilities to whatever unique constituencies—stockholders, voters, contributors, or beneficiaries—they serve. The megacommunity concept does not call for across-the-board agreement or startling new levels of selflessness. As Barbara Waugh, the director of University Relations at Hewlett-Packard (and the initiator of several megacommunity efforts) suggests, "The megacommunity approach takes advantage of self-interest. It doesn't require leaders of organizations to give up their drives for personal wealth, power, or status. Nor does it require organizations to forfeit their own objectives. Individuals and organizations come to megacommunities when they recognize that the problems facing them are more complex than they can solve alone."

The megacommunity is set up to gain energy and excitement, not enervation and exhaustion, from the "dynamic tension" that naturally exists among business, government, and civil society when they attempt to operate simultaneously in the same space. As Marjorie Yang, chairwoman and CEO of Esquel Enterprises Limited, one of the world's leading cotton apparel and textile manufacturers, expressed during one of our interviews, "The dynamic tension between the three parts constitutes a system that will accommodate growth and promote the quality of globalization."

This concept of dynamic tension, represented in the figure below, provides a simple but effective way to understand the interactions between the major global sectors that, if managed properly, will support the effectiveness of a megacommunity.

In a healthy megacommunity, the three sectors maintain balance by "pushing" and "pulling" at each other according to their respective forms of influence. Take, for example, the story of the Forestry Stewardship Council (FSC)—an international nonprofit organization founded in 1993 to support environmentally appropriate, socially beneficial, and economically viable management of the world's forests. In March 2006, it launched the FSC Controlled Wood Global Risk Registry program that will be funded by a two-year $380,000 grant from The Home Depot Foundation. The registry will help companies ensure that they purchase wood harvested in a responsible manner. What makes this program particularly relevant is the fact that just a few years earlier, the FSC was threatening Home Depot with boycotts because of its practice of selling wood coming from old-growth forests. As this example shows, the natural

FIGURE 2.1: THE DYNAMIC TENSIONS
INHERENT IN A MEGACOMMUNITY

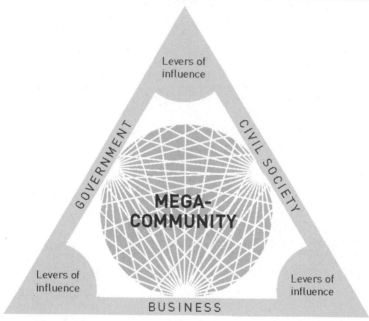

The concept of dynamic tension provides a simple but effective way to understand the interactions between the major global sectors that, if managed properly, will support the ability of the megacommunity to address its overlapping vital interests. As the figure shows, each sector connects to the other sectors through levers of influence (for example, regulations act as a lever of influence between government and business, boycotts act as a lever of influence between civil society and business, voting acts as a lever of influence between civil society and government) keeping in mind that levers of influence exist in both directions. Megacommunity protocols and principles create and maintain a *dynamic tension* between businesses, governments, and civil society as they attempt to operate simultaneously in the same space.

Source: Booz Allen Hamilton

tension within a megacommunity could be seen as going a long way toward sharpening each sector's sense of their own objectives within the overall mission. Just as no one corner of the triangle can be disconnected from the others, the responsibility for managing the activities of a megacommunity lies with no one sector in particular. It is shared by all.

In addition, when one element of the triangle unduly dominates the other two, the negative aspects and effects become evident to all. An interesting point here is that the negative power does not quash the ability of the other sectors to act—instead, it creates a form of feedback that redirects the negative energy back toward the "abuser." It is this effect that accounts for the way that huge multinational companies like Nike, BP, and Wal-Mart can be brought to their knees by an NGO. (For example, in June 2005, the *Wall Street Journal* ran a page-one story on the huge effect that one activist organization in California—with only one full-time employee—had on a large global beverage company. An executive from that company acknowledged that this nonprofit organization was a central figure in a burgeoning global campaign that "has cost it millions of dollars in lost sales and legal fees in India, and growing damage to its reputation elsewhere."[1]) To be effective, the megacommunity must represent and link the needs and perspectives of the three primary sectors. Order comes out of integrating and balancing the decision rights and roles of various players, that is, harnessing the dynamic tension.

The challenge for leaders in all three sectors is to find a way to channel—and sustain—this natural tension. As a result, megacommunity calls for an unprecedented amount of cross-sector dialogue. This was clearly missing, for example, in the case of Enel in Brindisi.

Articulating what has become a central tenet of megacommunity, Harvard University's John Ruggie says, "Life in the world of sustainable globalization is a permanent negotiation." A megacommunity is a vehicle for taking on permanent negotiation without being overwhelmed by it. We certainly saw the value of this approach in October 2003, when more than 200 professionals met in New Delhi with a common goal: to establish a coordinated approach for combating HIV/AIDS in India. The objective for this event, as we noted in the preface to this book, was to accelerate industry involvement in the fight against HIV/AIDS. The event was organized and sponsored by the Global Business Coalition on HIV/AIDS (GBC), Booz Allen Hamilton, and the Confederation of Indian Industry (CII). Representatives from all three sectors were present, as were the following: a global soft drink and food company; the Tata Group (the giant India-based conglomerate); the director of the HIV, TB, and reproductive health programs from the Gates Foundation; heads of local NGOs that worked with people in the cities, towns, and villages of India; health department members, executive officials, and senior military officers from the Indian government; senior leaders from the U.S. Department of Health and Human Services and the U.S. Agency for International Development (USAID); and leaders from the World Bank, several United Nations agencies, and the World Health Organization. People living with HIV/AIDS were represented by the community workers who work with them to manage the disease every day.

The event was designed as a strategic simulation, with participants grouped into teams representing major stakeholders. The teams were presented with the current state of HIV/AIDS in India and, during a series of three moves, worked together to address the spread of the epidemic in India. At the end of each move, teams briefed the entire group on their decisions, and the facilitation team quantified the public health and economic impact of the decisions using an integrated epidemiological and economic model. The simulation represented a ten-year span.

Coming into the event, the participants held no common view on how to slow the spread of the disease. But they all knew that, left unchecked, HIV/AIDS could undermine the future of the Indian economy, India's people, culture, and even the world's economy. Though no one used the word "megacommunity" at the time, the concept was emerging: To successfully stop the spread of HIV/AIDS in India, fragmented solutions would not be sufficient. With the limited time available, some kind of catalyst for a better mutual approach was needed.

The two-day simulation began with a great deal of contention. The participants knew how to do their own jobs well, and many had opinions about how others should do theirs. But the simulated crisis kept getting worse. No one had answers. People complained, pointed fingers, shouted at one another, and explained why each other's proposed solutions were impractical.

Then a small change took place. One team admitted that it needed another team's help: "Would the members of the federal government team be willing to flow the majority of funds to state regions where they are needed?" Another team followed suit: "Could we use corporate facilities to help others in the surrounding region?" And another: "Treatment options need to be linked with counseling, but the drugs are too expensive. . . . Could we develop lower-cost solutions together?" A group of NGOs created a new pool of jointly funded programs to lever-age their money and other resources more effectively.

Slowly, the group began to function as a megacommunity. Partici-pants started to address the shortcomings of traditional approaches to the issue, and they began to see the outline of a new type of "win–win" mindset. In the end, the 200-plus professionals generated ideas for a re-markable number of partnerships—54—that were focused on more than 100 separate initiatives.

These results were not restricted to the simulation. In the weeks that followed, Tata expanded its workplace and community activities to encourage effective HIV/AIDS prevention through mass awareness and education. The Lafarge Group and six other global companies (Anglo-American, Chevron Texaco, DaimlerChrysler, Eskom, Heineken, and Tata Steel) announced that they would use their facilities, employees, and other infrastructure to expand workplace HIV/AIDS prevention and treatment programs into the communities in which they operate. In early 2004, Cipla Ltd, an Indian pharmaceutical company, in con-junction with three other global drug companies and a global NGO, an-nounced an HIV/AIDS drug attainable for less than one dollar per day.[2] To this day, these organizations continue to talk and work together. They have formed an ongoing megacommunity.

It may seem, when skimming the surface of this example that megacommunities coalesce around a sense of social good or altruism. But what really brought folks to the table were hard-core issues such as HIV/AIDS's effect on India's GDP and productivity rates for business (certainly amplified by the possibility of achieving some social good).

The New Delhi example also underscores the fact that, in order to achieve a megacommunity-level of performance, new capabilities and a new kind of leadership are imperative.

There are many signs that leaders are beginning to recognize this fact. Writing in the *Financial Times* in 2006, Sam Palmisano, IBM chairman and chief executive, insisted that multinational companies must move away from what he described as their colonial approach—chastising companies that, for example, build factories in Europe and Asia while keeping all their research and development in the United States.[3] Similar concepts have emerged from leaders of such companies as GE, Unilever, and dozens of others. Government and civil society also echo this concern.

Of course, the need for full integration does not stop with the equitable transfer of business operations. As the New Delhi simulation shows, full integration must involve the flow of ideas and information along the entire megacommunity, taking in the widest array of identifiable stakeholders including business leaders, local officials, academics, environmentalists, and members of NGOs.

ESSENTIAL CONDITIONS FOR A MEGACOMMUNITY

We observe more and more examples of megacommunity-like activity occurring all the time. But such activity occurs in diffuse, partial, or emergent ways. Many popular, big ideas such as "Business Process Reengineering" and "Total Quality Management" developed slowly, but businesses could not employ them in a targeted fashion until a discipline was fully defined. The time has come to define the megacommunity phenomena both generally and in terms of practical application, so that leaders can more competently and confidently begin to move forward. Let's begin by taking a closer look at the defining conditions for megacommunity and its key features.

1) TRI-SECTOR ENGAGEMENT

The megacommunity concept goes far beyond such well-meaning single sector approaches as corporate social responsibility (CSR). A CSR initiative, while laudable, often represents the fulfillment of a perceived obligation or duty rather than a collective movement toward a mutual aim. In other words, CSR is limited by its unilateral, single-sector nature: The corporation sets the terms of its involvement as it seeks to meet the standards established by either government or civil society. But there is no real dialogue or exchange.

One way to compensate for this lack is through the formation of public–private partnerships. Most public–private partnerships are, in effect, deals struck between governments—or intergovernmental organizations such as the UN or NATO—and companies. Their purpose is typically to address some relatively circumscribed goal, the attainment of which requires both the government and private industry to play a part: for example, overseeing the design of a new mass transit system or vaccine distribution. Although public–private partnerships can be successful in certain, circumscribed, contract-oriented situations, they are limited by their bi-sector nature. As Melanne Verveer, chairwoman of Vital Voices Global Partnership, an international nonprofit that supports emerging women leaders in building vibrant democracies and strong economies, points out, "If globalization is completely driven by one or two actors with the third actor completely disregarded—that third actor being the vast numbers of people in civil society—then you've got a problem."

In contrast to public–private partnerships, megacommunities bring civil society into the equation. The megacommunity recognizes the kind of legitimacy that civil society represents. As Peter Eigen of Transparency International says, "While the state governments, the international institutions and the private sector can play an important role, they cannot do it alone. They don't have the credibility. They need the addition of strong civil society organizations." According to former President Bill Clinton, "The growth of NGOs was one of the great developments of the last two decades that is largely unremarked on. They need to be brought into the decision-making on government policies both in rich countries and the poor countries." Among other things, Clinton adds, "they can make up for a lot of the loss of government capacity. They can supplement the government."

In addition, civil society brings a different point of view and differentiated expertise on a given issue. They have the track record for actually dealing with the problems, and they can focus without either the bureaucratic restrictions or the profit motive. Moreover, expectations of increased transparency and the speed of information transfer continue to make civil society a bigger and stronger player—as we saw in Brindisi—making a tri-sector approach increasingly essential.

Examples of the tri-sector approach range in scale and scope, from planet-wide systems, such as the community of corporations, governments, and NGOs concerned with rainforest management and conservation, to local enterprise-related environments. One of the examples we know best is the Harlem Small Business Initiative—a case of local tri-sector engagement in action and an excellent model for megacommunity thinking.

In late 2001, a series of large chain retailers announced plans to open stores in several New York neighborhoods. A number of Harlem small business owners, fearing the impact of this kind of competition on their long-standing customer base, approached former President Clinton, who had recently set up offices for his new foundation in this uptown Manhattan locale, known globally as a center of African American culture. Sifting through the different types of help the storeowners might need, Clinton's foundation suggested that they make the existing Harlem businesses more competitive and capable. To foster this, he suggested that the owners create a new kind of partnership with not-for-profit status, calling on a wide range of organizations to help.

The storeowners themselves were enthusiastic about this; like the foundation staff, they recognized the limits of unilateral action. They founded a new organization called the Harlem Small Business Initiative, pulling in a large number of groups. The participating groups included the office of Harlem's U.S. Congressman, Charles Rangel, the Greater Harlem Chamber of Commerce, the Harlem Business Alliance, the Harlem Friends (a group of small businesses and citizens), the National Black MBA Association, New York University's Stern School of Business, and our own management consulting firm, Booz Allen Hamilton. These were not figurehead groups or silent sponsors; each invested a great deal of time, effort, and creativity in the project. But no single entity was "in charge," nor did the autonomous groups take orders from the Harlem Small Business Initiative. Instead, they worked out a way to participate together, defining mutual goals and establishing reasonable constraints on the overall system and then playing their parts individually.

A 22-month program was launched in mid-2002, focused on helping ten local businesses, including a plumber's storefront, a women's hat shop, a florist, a dentist's office, and a yoga center. The business owners were already good examples of local entrepreneurship; they loved their work and managed their businesses reasonably well. The plumber, for example, had put several kids through college. But there was definitely room for improvement. (For example, in some cases, receipts were kept in shoeboxes and, too often, phones went unanswered.) But, even with these improvements, they would be highly vulnerable to competition from larger retailers with citywide or national brand names.

Congressman Rangel's office and the various local business alliances helped the other Initiative participants understand the fabric of the community and the value of these small businesses as both employers and vendors. The MBA students, volunteer accountants, and management consultants taught business methods and marketing approaches. "We went in and created income statements and balance sheets from handwritten receipts that went back 10 years," said one participant. "Then we analyzed the customers, and how they had changed over time, and whether [the stores] would benefit by hiring more staff."

The result was wildly successful. While some large chain retailers, in-cluding Starbucks, Disney, and Old Navy, have entered Harlem, the Initia-tive is credited with helping to keep the original neighborhood vibrant and varied. An impressive number of the small businesses served by the Initiative doubled revenues and increased profitability within less than two years. Jobs were created, the tax base was enhanced, and the services to customers improved. As one entrepreneur said, "These kids are dedi-cating all this time. They're not getting any money for it. How dare I not get excited about moving my business ahead when they're so excited?"

In an earlier era, the Harlem Small Business Initiative might have ended up managed by one of the three sectors: a redevelopment agency, a neighborhood organization, or perhaps a business-funded partner-ship with a public- or civil-sector organization. It would not have been comprehensive, nor would it have brought people together across all three sectors; most likely, the results would have been limited by the skills and experience of the few participating organizations. By contrast, the megacommunity approach brought dozens of organizations to-gether on a single issue.

This megacommunity approach was so successful that in May 2004, a second phase started, with similar programs launched in Brooklyn and the Bronx. The Harlem Small Business Initiative has been renamed the Urban Enterprise Initiative, itself a measure of the applicability of megacommunity methods.

The Harlem Initiative example demonstrates the specific capabili-ties that each sector typically brings to the megacommunity. Business—or the private sector—brings a resource base, an action agenda, depth in problem solving, and capital. Government brings the rule of law, the promise of long-term stability, sovereignty, a tax base, and natural resources. The civil sector brings accountability, insight into how to get things done locally, sensitivity to how the issues at play might affect individuals and the environment, and credibility in arenas in which business and government fall short. As Melanne Verveer of Vital Voices succinctly states, "The [megacommunity] triangle is equivalent to a three-legged stool. If one leg is shorter, you have an imbalance, and if one leg is chopped off, you can't sit on the stool."

Involvement in a megacommunity allows any participating part of any sector to utilize the abilities, the knowledge, and even the prejudices of the other sectors. Working together, there is the potential for a kind of "swarm intelligence" to emerge, one that allows you to create innovative ideas, generate new energy around the topic, identify different ways of approaching the issue, and—last but not least—have more participants available to do what needs to be done. In that way, it echoes what Ken Chenault of American Express sees as a preferred state. "If [the] focus is on, 'How can I use the resources of a particular global power to accelerate my progress and, as a partner, have some say in ultimately what my destiny should be'—that is a major plus!"

2) AN OVERLAP IN VITAL INTERESTS

One of the built-in ironies of the megacommunity idea is that, most likely, you are already part of one without realizing it. In fact, you may be part of several. Although active megacommunities are consciously developed, as in the case of the Harlem Initiative, they usually grow out of the latent megacommunities that are all around us. Before the involvement of the Clinton Foundation, the small business environment of Harlem could certainly have been seen as a latent megacommunity.

It is important to understand that being a part of a megacommunity is not really an elective choice. Megacommunities, latent or active, exist when the following features are present:

A Shared Issue

Members of a megacommunity do not necessarily need to have the same objectives, but they must share a problem (climate change, the threat of terrorism), resource availability (oil, water, the Amazon rainforest), or aspiration (education, health care, enhanced business interaction). Everything starts with some shared issue—which is why, depending on their mission and/or operations, all organizations are "de facto" members of megacommunities. In most of these situations, individual organizations cannot opt out of their megacommunity unless they change their mission. As long as, say, you are there to fight HIV/AIDS in Africa, and are affected in some way by the HIV/AIDS issue, then you are automatically part of that megacommunity. You can choose how much to participate, and you can choose the form of your participation. But even if you don't show up, you are still a member, and your absence or lack of contribution will be noted.

A Shared Sense of Impact

A megacommunity not only forms around a problem but also around those areas where the impact is felt—and that impact can come from the inside or outside. The shared problem is often local; indeed, some of the examples we know best are geographically specific. The Harlem megacommunity grew up around a pre-existing need in the community at large. The Florida response to Hurricane Andrew stretched as far as Tallahassee, and barely made it to Biloxi, but never quite reached to New Orleans. (In the next few years, as the Gulf Coast develops a megacommunity-style approach to emergency preparedness, that may change.) But shared local geography is not always a prerequisite. Since technology has allowed the rapid transfer of money, images, ideas, and people around the world, "local" communities are neither constrained nor protected by age-old boundaries of geography and demography. A vendor in a remote village in Costa Rica or Bangladesh is bound, through communication, trade, and an increasing number of common interests, with an urban resident of Paris or Hong Kong. While Enel in Brindisi is a geographically specific case, the efforts of Enel in general can be seen as part of a much larger latent megacommunity—one the size of all of Europe, at least, and intimately connected with the ebb and flow of worldwide energy alternatives. Keeping this in mind, all latent megacommunities—no matter how global—can be seen as growing up around issues that are "local" or have localized impact.

Together, shared issues and shared impact naturally result in an overlap of vital interests. And depending on the nature of the problem, megacommunities can be the most effective way to bring these interests into workable, sustainable alignment.

3) CONVERGENCE

Before an active megacommunity begins to coalesce, there must be more than a floating overlap of interests. There must be a convergence of commitment toward mutual action. It is as if, like a stone rolling down a hill, a latent megacommunity must convert its potential energy into kinetic motion.

This convergence may happen spontaneously, as in the case of a natural disaster, when there is a sudden intensification of need. But most likely, convergence will occur when each separate constituency affected by any issue realizes that its progression has achieved a plateau or roadblock, when any additional effort does not produce further improvement.

An individual organization may be able to jump-start a megacommunity, but only when leaders of diverse organizations within the latent megacommunity consciously engage together does a true megacommunity begin to take shape. In fact, as the Harlem Initiative shows, a nascent megacommunity may not even contain all the members it needs at first. In that case, the need to reach out for additional and complementary support becomes a necessity—which is to say that megacommunities evolve as the issue expands or contracts. Although tools such as the Internet enable more channels of communication among the three sectors, the members do not normally come together on an active megacommunity level of their own accord. They are kept apart by their own constituents, by the aspects of their goals that are at cross-purposes, and by their perceptions of each other. If active complete megacommunities did spontaneously evolve, we would have many more today than we do. Their scarcity is a clear indication that they need both a deliberate catalyst and a fundamental formula.

Whenever convergence does occur, the evidence is a shift in the capabilities of the community. Instead of continuing to fight each other or to cede authority to some governmental or quasi-governmental body, leaders come together as equals to develop a plan of action. One cannot participate in a megacommunity with the intent to disrupt or undermine the effort to move the overlapping vital interests forward. The commitment toward mutual action must be genuine or the megacommunity will not work.

4) CROSS-ORGANIZATIONAL STRUCTURES

For a megacommunity to operate effectively there needs to be an explicit formative process, grounded in a set of protocols and organizing principles that bring a degree of order to the relationships among the organizations, before their differences harden into conflicting interests. There must be an agreement to use these protocols based on some sense of mission alignment. And these protocols must allow for the best use of "dynamic tension." The wargame on HIV/AIDS in India was exactly that kind of process—condensed into two days.

Interestingly, the structure of a megacommunity—based as it is on overlapping issues—exhibits many properties of a network. The shift from the bilateralism of a public–private partnership to the tri-sector nature of a megacommunity takes us automatically into a complex, networked environment. Becoming part of a complex network is not only a natural outcome of tri-sector engagement. It's a welcome one since the structures of high-performing networks provide precedents for ways to truly galvanize participation and boost productivity.

A network structure, like a hierarchy, is simply a recurring pattern of communications among people. But where a hierarchy is constructed with formal, tiered relationships, in which each person is defined by their accountability to the tiers above them, a network is depicted by mapping recurring patterns of unstructured contact. Hierarchies do not in themselves allow people to easily exchange knowledge or inspire trust. Networks do.

Networks of human communication, like networks of computer-based communication, can be mapped and analyzed mathematically, by capturing the relationships and information flows in terms of "nodes" (the points of connections) and "links" (that which connect the nodes).

Since the 1970s, the field of social network analysis (inspired both by anthropological research, sociological theory, and by electronic network analysis) has added greatly to our understanding of the flow of knowledge in a community.

For example, Stanford University Professor Mark Granovetter became famous for demonstrating the "strength of weak ties": that is, it isn't necessary to know someone deeply, or well, to allow for the exchange of the kind of information that makes the whole system more productive. Weak ties bring information into the network that is not provided by the members with "strong" ties. Indeed, people with many "weak ties" (or casual and temporary acquaintances) are often better informed and better equipped to share information than people with a few "strong ties" to close friends and family members.

One important insight from social network analysis is the value of diversity: Communities that acknowledge and tap into differences are generally more successful than those that cling to homogeneity. Smaller, tighter networks are less useful to their members than networks with lots of loose connections (Granovetter's "weak ties") to individuals out-side the main network. As the Harlem Initiative proved, the need to reach out for complementary support is an essential factor in making megacommunities highly adaptable and "scale-free" (that is, they can escalate at will, using certain key nodes as anchor points in the same way shopping malls use large department stores and movie theaters as primary attractors). Typically, megacommunities will form "open net-works," with many weak ties and social connections through which their members are more likely to introduce new ideas and opportuni-ties, as opposed to closed networks with many redundant "strong ties."

Experience suggests that megacommunity leaders must develop a better understanding of network forces, in addition to market forces. Networked operating models continue to jump to the forefront as or-ganizations seek to improve efficiency and effectiveness. Networks are being used to achieve radical new levels of organizational integration and performance. Understood as a network, a megacommunity can have the same result.

5) ADAPTABILITY

Consider the static nature of most public–private partnerships (PPPs). In order to negotiate a working relationship, both sides expect to isolate the issue upon which they agree and set rules around engagement on the issue. Thus, when conflicts or new issues arise, PPPs do not gener-ally allow for flexible responses. The terms of engagement have been set from the start, and the design has deliberately excluded change because that would be seen as collusion or abandonment of principle. The relationship is locked down.

Megacommunities, on the other hand, are designed to be dynamic. This starts with their tri-sector nature but it is embodied in the built-in mutability of their processes, and in their goal of sustainable results; since nothing long-term can be predicted absolutely, expectations of adaptability must be set from the start. Adaptability is sustainability. Specific goals and objectives are subject to change. Robert Switz, president and CEO of ADC Telecommunications, Inc. calls for "a constant re-evaluation of what it is that we're involved in and the nature of this globalization that we're working towards. We should be testing one's thoughts on that on a regular basis." A healthy megacommunity is up to that challenge.

Over time, a healthy megacommunity becomes more effective in its purpose. With sustained connections and continued interactions, the members of megacommunities develop bonds, intellectual pathways, enhanced linguistic abilities, and even a higher capacity for critical thinking and problem-solving around the set of vital interests that prompted the megacommunity to form in the first place.

The adaptation within a megacommunity occurs naturally, without hierarchical decision making and external intervention. The system constantly evolves and changes, in the same way that a living entity does. The evolution is not guided by command and control. Instead, things happen through alignment, through the collective behavior of all the members.

In a computer network, for example, when information packets coursing through a computer are smashing into each other and overflowing each other's buffers, causing overall performance to go down, the network has an adaptive capability that kicks in and adjudicates the problem. This is not caused by a centralized decision-making system—it is a distributed capability operating as an integral part of the network. The concept of megacommunity introduces a similar sort of network management mechanism, one that minimizes friction over time, and causes the efficiency of the entire network to improve. With no central decision-making entity and no explicit single leader of the megacommunity, everyone within the megacommunity has some influence.

An observer might reasonably wonder why a comfortable chief executive or head of a government agency or NGO would be interested in operating in a "control-free zone" in the first place. But transcending the need for central control is a common situation in large, complex systems (such as electrical power grids or environmental control systems). In fact, optimal network structures represent a shift from what are called bounded networks (with central control) to unbounded networks. Unbounded networks are characterized by distributed administrative control, combining previously fragmented operations into more focused processes open to many organizational participants.

Megacommunities do not thrive on chaos with no clear leadership. They thrive on alignment and optimization. In the initial stages in particular, the network needs some person, group, or sector to precipitate alignment and catalyze latent energies. This will generally take the form of some "initiator" (or group of initiators) doing something explicit to put the elements in place. But that initiator must be prepared to cede this central/initial leadership role as the megacommunity coalesces and grows, or they may be seen as co-opting local or other interests. Of course, each sector and specific organization involved continues to have its own leadership in place, and there will be leaders of groups assigned to furthering and monitoring megacommunity interaction. Still, no one possesses the title of "CEO of the megacommunity."

In the next three chapters, we will discuss in detail the nature of megacommunity thinking, as well as operating models and practical dynamics. We will delve deeper into each of the five features of mega-community: tri-sector engagement, overlap of vital interests, convergence, structure, and adaptability. And we will show that the recognition of these dynamics represents a new starting point for mutual action on a local and global scale. Considering problems through this sort of lens can profoundly influence the types of questions that leaders ask themselves before moving forward with any new enterprise, and it can also profoundly affect the ability of each leader to implement successfully the answers.

CHAPTER THREE

MEGACOMMUNITY THINKING

When facing complex problems, leaders worldwide have a pretty good sense of what doesn't work when it comes to innovative ideas. Some of the more extreme new approaches to "simplifying" complexity include using Internet betting to identify high probability outcomes, linking decisions to a "wisdom of crowds" idea. Author Jean-François Rischard has suggested gathering experts on particular topics and literally putting them on an island for a few years, hoping they will emerge with solutions. More down-to-earth solutions include looking for the person with authority in the area of concern to create some sort of governmental or even world governmental organization that can solve these problems from the top.

Such ideas arise and then, quite rightfully, get shot down. Given the convoluted nature of so many new challenges, there is no reason to think that the wisdom of crowds, the wisdom of experts, the wisdom of authority, or any other concentrated wisdom will be adequate to solve any of these problems.

What, then, do we know has worked? Interestingly, it all goes back to anthropologist Margaret Mead and her famous statement about never doubting that a small group of thoughtful, committed citizens can change the world—indeed, she tells us, it is the only thing that ever has.

When a group of leaders from organizations committed to a problem come together to solve that problem, we see dramatic progress—assuming they are inclusive enough, dedicated enough, and have some sort of process in place for making change happen. In some respects, the purpose of this book is to make that claim and to answer the following question: If it is true that you need a committed group of people from relevant and invested organizations, what then do you have to do to bring them into place and set them into motion? But before we start discussing action plans, we need to talk about the kinds of thinking—the theoretical underpinnings—that lead to action in a megacommunity.

A megacommunity is not only a mechanism—or set of mechanisms—for achieving success in increasingly complex local, regional, and global environments. It is also a mindset. The tenets of that mindset are relatively universal, while the particular measures or practices are myriad, and change to fit the situation at hand. Involvement in a megacommunity represents a positive developmental process for everyone that's in it. That's the context of the megacommunity: solving problems by building everyone's capabilities to think about those problems together.

Megacommunity thinking marks a transition point away from the standard levers of influence, protocols, and assumptions currently in practice by all three sectors. Many Western business principles, for example, were born in the era of big oil, big steel, and big banking. These ideals were rooted in control and developed during a time when information proliferation was very limited. The quintessential organizational phrase of that era was "vertically integrated." Large organizations strove for high degrees of central control over all critical business elements, placing them within easy reach of the chief executive. One reason for this tight, centralized approach was the difficulty in getting (and sharing) information. For reasons of efficiency and effectiveness, information and decision rights were concentrated in a central place. When it came time for big oil, big steel, and big banking to act, this high concentration of information gave them a tremendous advantage. But in today's interconnected world, information is more readily available, empowering everyone from potential business rivals to the curious civilian. And many organizations can no longer afford the cost associated with vertical integration—moving instead toward outsourcing and the use of external suppliers.

Yet, to a large degree, we are still living with these traditional business principles today—and with the models they use to define growth and success. By and large, each sector continues to pursue its mission as if very little has changed, failing to reflect our current environment of complexity and simultaneity. These changes that the megacommunity recognizes are revolutionary in scope and nature. And they require both new behaviors and fresh ways of thinking.

The tenets of "megacommunity thinking" do not necessarily replace the assumptions and attitudes that are prevalent *within* any single organization. These new forms of thinking can coexist with, even build on top of, existing organizational cultures—and connect them to the outside world. Nonetheless, entering into the megacommunity zone requires a renewed level of openness, determination, and mettle. It calls for some profound adjustments in attitude on the part of participating individuals, especially those in active leadership or liaison roles. And as such, it requires a disentangling of some deeply entrenched and ingrained habits of thought.

LEARNING TO OPTIMIZE

To achieve a successful megacommunity, one of the most fundamental habits to change is the habit of "maximizing" benefits. Megacommunity members must learn to "optimize" instead. "Maximizing" refers to a primary focus on the immediate benefits to your own local domain—either your own organization, your own geographic region, or your own function—whether or not that leads to benefits for the whole. "Optimizing" refers to the recognition and actualization of benefits to the larger system as a whole. When you're driving in heavy traffic, and you indulge in tailgating (following closely behind the car in front of you) or shifting from lane to lane, you are maximizing the system; you may well get to your destination a few minutes sooner than you otherwise would. But you're making the whole system suboptimal. When more than a few cars follow too closely or shift lanes too frequently, traffic jams become more likely because of the "wave" phenomena involved. All it takes is for one driver to slam on his or her brakes, and every driver in the queue behind will slam on the brakes as well, and the flow of traffic will lock up.

A driver caught in a traffic jam may fume about the lost time but the only way to really solve the problem is to stop tailgating, recognizing that every driver's fate is interconnected during the time they share that space. In many ways, "optimize not maximize" is the Golden Rule of megacommunities.

The history of human society is littered with many examples of one individual, sector, or organization maximizing their own benefits, without regard for the consequence to others, and succeeding in the short term—while undermining their true goals in the long run. In the sphere of government, maximizing advantage has been a perennial form of wisdom, from Plato's *Republic* to Sun Tzu's *Art of War* to Machiavelli's *The Prince* to modern-day concepts of realism and realpolitik in international relations. Maximizing played a decisive role in everything from the fall of the Roman Empire to contemporary business case study examples like the Enron debacle, or Nestlé's infant formula operations in Africa (where an apparent lack of sensitivity to local perspective on breast feeding became a public relations nightmare).

The maximizing mindset is not limited to the business and government sectors. A well-known story is the case of the decommissioning of the Brent Spar Oil Rig in the North Sea, between England and Norway. The massive oil platform had been built in the North Sea by Shell UK in 1976, but eventually, its drilling field became essentially tapped out. In 1995, after an exhaustive environmental and financial impact study, Shell UK decided the most effective disposal method for the rig was to tow it to a 2 km deep mid-ocean trough off the coast of Scotland, and sink it. This was expected to cost £17–20 million, affect the waters minimally (about 10,000 fish might be affected), and have minimal impact on Shell's employees. Despite the presence of hazardous waste, the seabed would recover in 12–14 months. The second-best alternative would cost £41 million, and involve towing the rig to Yrkefjorden harbor in Norway where it would be dismantled piece-by-piece and the hazardous waste disposed of professionally on land. Assuming all went well, adverse impact on either the environment or the workers from the second option would also be minimal. Both plans had been approved by the respective governments involved—the UK approved sinking the rig off the coast of Scotland, and Norway approved the Yrkefjorden plan.

From Shell UK's standpoint, the sinking plan seemed optimal. From an environmental standpoint, the options would be nearly equal in impact. Factoring in the increased complexity of the second option, the sinking option was also the most cost- and operationally-effective.

Two months after the local authority (the Scottish Fisheries Research Services) granted permission for the sinking plan, Greenpeace— who had been involved in the process all along—took action. Apparently uncomfortable with the outcome, it launched a public critique, arguing (falsely, it turns out) that the hazardous waste on the rig would have severe environmental impacts if it were sunk. The resulting protests culminated in a high-profile occupation of the derelict rig by members of the German branch of Greenpeace. A massive global boycott of Shell followed in the wake of the occupation as did negative media attention. This was enough to convince Shell's leaders to change their plans and opt for land-based decommissioning after all—even though that may not have been the best plan.

Greenpeace looked at the situation exclusively through its lens and realized their constituency would only want the Yrkefjorden plan, regardless of other factors. Shell's scientists always maintained that the deep-sea disposal would have had as little, or less, environmental impact. In fact, Greenpeace's claims of the toxicity of the platform were later discredited, and Lord Melchett, the executive director of Greenpeace UK, later published an apology in *The New Scientist*.

Maximizing has been at the heart of some of the most successful corporate strategic approaches, from the marketplace plurality of Wal-Mart and Tesco, to the technological hegemonies of Microsoft and Google. Each of these companies succeeded by, in effect, using its position as the dominant supplier of a certain kind of product to set prices or provide services that rivals couldn't match. Each used its influence to shore up its own position, making it more difficult for rivals to function and, ultimately, survive. Each took its own growth as a priority over the growth and survival of a more diverse, robust industry of competitors and entrepreneurs. And each prospered accordingly.

What, then, is wrong with maximization? It turns out to be an ineffective strategy when seeking to solve complex problems that have multi-sector roots and ramifications, and that lie beyond the reach of any individual group, organization, or nation. In a megacommunity, in other words, maximization turns out to produce minimal results.

Marjorie Yang, chairwoman and CEO of Esquel Enterprises, points out that "issues exist on the global scale that could undermine business and government if not properly collectively managed: the environment, health, microeconomic issues." And if we accept the premise that there are global challenges that inherently affect all three sectors, we must recognize that no one sector—or actor within that sector—possesses all the capabilities to meet these challenges. The notion that working together is anathema to "good business" or "good government" or "good stewardship" is something that megacommunity thinking confronts directly.

When leaders within the sectors recognize and include the goals and objectives of the other sectors (and even their rivals within their sectors) in their planning of a megacommunity strategy—that is, when they engage in "optimizing" behavior—the result is an overall strengthening of each sector. The net result is that the three sectors create a system of aggregate capabilities that allows them all to maintain the ability to achieve their own goals over the long term, by doing what they do best. By pooling capabilities and optimizing the benefit of criss-crossing agendas, instead of maximizing their own individual agendas, the benefits to each are sustained for a longer period of time.

More and more, we are seeing encouraging examples of combined capabilities at work, from which we might begin to derive new strategies. In our discussions with former President Clinton, he offered one already-influential example: the disbursement of antiretroviral medicines (necessary for treatment of HIV/AIDS) in Brazil. "Brazil is the only developing country where 100% of the people who need antiretrovirals get them," he says. "The government has a pharmaceutical industry that can produce those drugs generically for the Brazilian population. The medicine, however, is handed out by a remarkable combination of public partnerships. The government is involved. The Catholic Church is involved. And all these NGOs are involved.

"So you've got people taking this medicine properly way up in the Amazon River Valley, in indigenous tribes that don't even speak Portuguese. And the government could not have done it alone. The government provided the medicine but the government could not have had the delivery system. There's no way in the world that this work could be done quickly in these developing countries without the involvement of NGOs that are both indigenous to the country and from the outside."

Opening your mind to the concept of optimization calls for a major shift in thinking, away from a pervasive and nearly primal philosophy, held as inviolable in many circles: "Winner takes all." By their very nature, maximizers follow a zero-sum strategy. They can only win if everyone else loses. They do not need to see everyone else destroyed; it's enough for them if all the other rivals and participants have lesser status, or a much more constrained playing field.

In a world where local domination is possible, this strategy can be effective. But in more complex situations or global circumstances, "winner takes all" has proven to be a highly unstable and unsustainable course. The simple fact is that without reasonable competition, capabilities do not evolve and companies often atrophy. As a consequence, companies lack the drive and product and business innovation to keep them at the top of their game. Success is fleeting unless you continuously improve and evolve.

In fact, the day may soon come when those of the "winner takes all" mindset find themselves completely stranded. As Yang gibes, "You want to be the winner who takes all? Hey, you won't have anybody left to play ball with you. The other players are going to be gone. Would you rather be left playing by yourself? Or do you really want to play and have a good time? This is a very important concept."

Optimizing behavior accepts the reality that unilateralism is a thing of the past. This is not only the result of altruism or heightened social consciousness. It's a realistic response to the recognition of our interdependence. "We just have to have a broader view of what our self-interest is," says Paul Leonard, former CEO of Habitat for Humanity International. "It's in everybody's self-interest to be the keeper of the community, to create conditions where people can live healthy lives and have the opportunity to grow and prosper. It can't just be for the employees of your company, or for your shareholders. It has to be for the human community, if it's going to be sustainable."

Others talk about reciprocity as a strategic goal. "There are lots of things corporations can do, for example, but I don't think it should ever be viewed as charitable," says Clinton. "Whether you take on education or health care or economic development or government capacity or the absence of clean water, everything should be done from an empowerment model." And in a megacommunity, empowerment does not only flow to those who are getting the help but to those who are giving the help too.

SENSING AND AWARENESS

Optimizing may be the central tenet of megacommunity thinking, but it can't work if you don't understand your partners and arrive at that understanding in a timely fashion. Leaders need to anticipate in order to inform, educate, steer, and reach consensus. Megacommunities start with an understanding, with a commitment to achieving a heightened sensitivity to differences in motives and values. Members of a mega-community—especially its leaders and liaisons—function most effectively in a listening, learning mode. While most leaders know how to sense the needs of their own organizations, participation in a megacommunity requires its members to tune their antennae more broadly, in order to pick up subtle signals from the outside world. As Robert Switz, president and CEO of ADC Telecommunications Inc., says, "You simply have to begin that painful process of running your organization with many more constituencies than you've traditionally focused upon."

This broader set of constituencies creates an imperative to be more adaptive. An adaptive system, like a megacommunity, is a system that is able to modify and adjust its behavior in response to changes in the environment or in parts of the system itself. Control systems for electric utilities are great examples of this—they use feedback loops in order to sense the conditions in their environment and make adjustments as needed to keep the power flowing.

Sensing and awareness to support adaptivity is necessary all the way up and down the line in a megacommunity setting. It produces leaders who can perceive the first behavioral signs and attitudes that would allow for the engagement of the other sectors. It allows them to sense the general desire to "megacommunitize." It allows them to perceive the possibility and requirements of convergence. And it is imperative when seeking the answer to what John Ruggie of Harvard University offers as one of megacommunity's central challenges: "What do you converge behind?"

1) SENSING ACROSS BORDERS

To begin to answer John Ruggie's all-important question, those involved in the megacommunity must appreciate the importance of building network capital (that is, the value of the investment in relationships and connections). Yet despite our interconnectedness, network capital is not so easy to come by. We must recognize that network capital is only valuable if it aligns with the objective function or value structure of the other players in our megacommunity. What's valuable to you may not be valuable to them. What's seen as "capital" to you may have little or no currency with them. Truly valuable network capital has to be built over time. It cannot be created instantaneously. And it must be built deliberately and thoughtfully with a keen sense of the other guy's value system, taking into account that a value system is not always static.

This is especially true for megacommunities that propagate to different geographies, such as those dealing with health issues like HIV/AIDS and malaria, or scientific issues like genetic engineering, or social concerns like women's right and homosexuality. And in this rapidly interconnecting world, it's just as dangerous to assume alignment as it is to disregard alignment. Another country's value system is not always as obvious as it seems. "Adopt the attitude of a student and don't be too quick to preach," suggests George Yong-Boon Yeo, Singapore's minister of Foreign Affairs. "If you think you are there to teach before you have learned, you will fail." Megacommunity members must be prepared to recognize the validity of other value systems—although that does not mean they necessarily have to adopt it. As Yeo continues, "Each person has a deep nature which you cannot completely change. Yet the most important first step is understanding the nature of the participants."

Certainly, cultural insensitivity is one of the major blocks to establishing a megacommunity—and it can be detected across the board. Cultural misapprehensions are evident in the business sector (such as those that colored the Enel/Brindisi affair). They're apparent in the government sector. (Consider, briefly, the U.S. policy bungles in Iraq.) And—perhaps surprisingly to some—they manifest with some regularity in the civil sector. For example, in the late 1990s, ApproTEC, a nongovernmental organization (NGO), ran into trouble when developing a water pump to be used by Kenyan small farmers. Although they eventually succeeded in selling more than 24,000 pumps in Kenya and Tanzania, their first design needed to be readdressed when women using the pump found themselves "in culturally unacceptable positions" while drawing water. So the pump was redesigned to allow the women to work the pump with their legs closer together to accommodate this cultural factor. ApproTEC's experience illustrates the need for an extremely fine-tuned set of antennae. You must do your best to sense and address all the cultural repercussions that can be anticipated—if only because there are so many that can never be anticipated.[1]

Probing deeply into any community—its actors, its roles, its needs, its ambitions—will naturally aid in bypassing stereotypes. And it will make the members of the megacommunity more able to traverse changes in the political, economic, and social landscapes of their partners. It's important to remember that the socioeconomic and political characteristics of each geography go a long way toward determining the typology of any given megacommunity.

The megacommunity's ability to take action is deeply affected by such factors as the maturation of the private sector, the strength of the NGO structure, and the level of commitment to the rule of law over the rule of the individual. And it is also imperative to key your eye on the more subtle changes that occur in the cultural sphere. As Pablo de la Flor, Peru's vice minister of international trade, points out, regarding Peru: "The way we construct culture is shifting and changing in leaps and bounds. It's a constantly moving situation. It's a very important element and it gets very little attention. And it may be the most important component of globalization." Making a commitment to sensing and awareness is the first step toward developing an in-depth set of practices that are responsive to these differences and mutations.

2) SENSING ACROSS SECTORS

Like crossing borders, crossing sectors comes with its own set of pitfalls. But sensing and awareness can go a long way toward building bridges. And key to this construction is the identification of value in the other sectors where you might not have seen it before. The business and government sectors must realize, for example, that NGOs are something to be valued and nurtured. It does not help anyone's cause to consider NGOs an annoyance or a roadblock to be overcome with corporate power. Pointing to one potential asset of engaging NGOs, Peter Eigen, founder of Transparency International, explains, "In a market where their competitors are not constrained from doing the wrong thing, it is very hard for them to uphold a very high standard, and therefore we find very often the corporate decision makers are in a dilemma. They are afraid that a person who takes the first steps to behave socially more responsible, will be punished for it, will be penalized. And therefore, I believe it is in the interest—the enlightened self-interest—of corporations to try to do coalitions with other actors that are able to create an improvement of the overall standards of social responsibility and yet maintain the level playing field."

Eigen goes so far as to suggest that "civil society organizations like Transparency International should try to dream up solutions that offer that escape route from the prisoner's dilemma in which many of the actors find themselves." That kind of thinking could lead the NGO community out of its own set of thinking traps. In the NGO community, sensing and awareness should play a key role in identifying that time and place when shouting should convert to constructive engagement. And it should help the civil sector expand its own view of the business sector's potential contribution. As John Ruggie says, "It's hard for non-business actors to look at business fundamentally as anything other than a source of funds. What they would really like are checks. Rare is the other social actor who has a good sense of business's institutional resources, human resources, the skills that a business can bring to the table."

Sensing and awareness also helps the sectors get past certain thinking traps that are anathema to megacommunity. They can help overcome certain forms of hubris (as in, "I am doing this for their own good") and defeatism (whereby a problem is considered intractable— an attitude that often pops up in civil service). None of these attitudes are very helpful in a megacommunity—but we cite them with the knowledge that, as leaders drive their own objectives, a megacommunity can be a tough arena to be in.

As we've mentioned in previous chapters, each sector in a megacommunity offers a different value proposition to its constituencies. And there exists the perception that this "value" puts them on a collision course. We don't believe that these values are necessarily in opposition. But in the spirit of sensing and awareness, a somewhat closer look at the differences between sectors is in order.

First of all, each sector's separate "mission" inevitably leads to the development of separate skill sets. In business, skills are generally co-linear with financial rewards, more capitalistic. The skills within the civil society sector, for example within an NGO, are more in line with altruism, while government sector skills are more polemical. And these skill sets result in what might be termed a different "language." Generally, language is more direct in private sector, more intricate in public sector, and more passionate and idiosyncratic in an NGO.

Each sector's internal cultures are also dissimilar, as they establish different types of responsibility, authority, and communication necessary to empower people to act in support of their particular mission. Much of this is derived from the decisions taken with regard to their governance structure, and governance structure varies in each of the three sectors.

The term "governance" deals with the processes and systems by which an organization operates. Governance implies the administrative and process-oriented activities that institutions use. It encompasses their structures of authority, their modes of collaboration, and their allocation of resources. In other words, it coordinates and controls their activity.

The three sectors all employ governance as described above, but they do so in very different ways. In general, governance in governments occurs through top–down methods that primarily involve bureaucracies. Businesses employ governance structures that make use of market mechanisms, where market principles of competition are used to allocate resources while operating under government regulation. Civil society uses both of these methods to some extent, but it also creates governance structures through networks involving partnerships with government agencies or with the collaboration of other community organizations. (Further complicating the issue, it's important to remember that the civil society sector is not solely comprised of activists. It represents an entire panoply of actors—media, religion, labor, and academia. They must all be addressed, not just the squeakiest wheels.)

All of these differences play a role in keeping the sectors apart. But when they remain apart, no one benefits. This tendency for separate sectors to operate as separate "nodes" tends to maximize autonomy, encourage isolation, and spread distrust or fear of working together. It leaves them looking for "zero-sum" situations—meaning, instances in which a participant's gain or loss is exactly balanced by the losses or gains of the other participants. (Cutting a cake, for example, is a zero-sum endeavor because taking a larger piece reduces the amount of cake available for others.) In the zero-sum equation, it is impossible for both players to win—which circles us back, once again, to the necessity of optimization in the megacommunity.

PATTERN STUDY

Megacommunity thinking not only requires that individuals use and develop their own awareness. They must be prepared to build awareness across the megacommunity—an awareness that reflects not only the founding mission, goals, terms, and conditions of engagement, but also an awareness of how to handle what might be in the megacommunity's future.

Behaviors in a complex system cannot be reliably predicted, but they can be understood. One of the main ways we can employ "sensing and awareness" is to stop looking for causes and start looking for patterns. Simple rules underlie even the most complex phenomena. Orienting your sensing and awareness efforts to finding patterns is an effective way to deal with unexpected change.

This potential for unexpected change is an inherent characteristic of our global network—the interconnectedness certainly makes us more productive, but at the same time it leaves us more vulnerable. The more interconnected we become, the greater the potential impact associated with disruptions. In short, we are trading predictability for efficiency. There is a certain comfort level that comes with knowing what will happen when a set of actions are taken—like playing chess and planning three or four moves in advance. That comfort level is challenged in today's complex world. It is getting harder and harder to predict behaviors, and even harder to anticipate consequences. Think of these examples of the aforementioned "butterfly effect" from newspaper headlines of the past few years:

- Nick Leeson, a rogue trader in Singapore, ran up £860m ($1.4 billion) in dealing losses and single-handedly brought down the global investment firm, Barings.
- Tree branches fell on power lines in Ohio triggering cascading effects leading to the largest electric power blackout in North American history, leaving more than 50 million people without power in eight states and parts of Canada.
- The decision taken by the city of Toronto to impose a virtual quarantine after an outbreak of SARS hit the local economy with an estimated $500-million impact and caused travel and business disruptions across the globe.

As all these examples show, specific events (e.g., the actions of a single trader, falling branches, a local quarantine) can create unpredictable reverberations through complex networks that, in turn, can result in major—even catastrophic—consequences.

In a more complex operating environment, actions must be addressed in the highly networked, interconnected context from which they emerged. The result is that we can no longer think only in terms of long-term planning and predictability, but also in terms of continuous sensing and awareness.

As an example, consider a story of success and failure in the face of a disruption within a complex network. A Nordic telecommunications company and its primary competitor, another European manufacturer, both depended on the same Koninklijke Philips Electronics NV semi-conductor plant in New Mexico for chips to power their mobile phones. But when a fire broke out at the factory in March 2000, the supply chain was disrupted. The Nordic company's officials had designed a system that sensed changes across their supply chain and therefore they noticed the problem even before being told that a plant had gone down. The pattern of activity had been disrupted—this anomaly was detected and tracked, and when it became clear that something was amiss, the company took action. Its chief supply troubleshooter immediately put together a team of 30 supply chain experts to fan out across Europe, Asia, and the United States to patch together a solution. They redesigned chips, accelerated a project to boost production, and used the company's clout to obtain more chips from other suppliers.

Eventually the other company became aware of the fire but couldn't connect the event with the impact. Without a sensing system built into its supply network, this company came up millions of chips short of the supply needed to launch a critical new product. The result, according to the *Wall Street Journal:* The Nordic company's market share grew by 3 percent; the competitor's dropped by the same amount. Before long, the other company withdrew from the handset market.[2]

The complexity within the megacommunity, like the telecommunications example, is not chaotic. In a complex system mindset, pattern study is not simply about knowing the past and linearly constructing the future based on those variables. It is about having a sense for how a system functions, what inputs or alliances could cause them to make great leaps, and who the important nodes are. This "mental feel" for the dynamics of a system allows for a much more accurate prediction of the future. Moreover, it allows companies to shape their future. Pattern study helps to determine which possible scenario a megacommunity may be heading toward, and which indicators may be most important to forecasting change. In this regard, the function of pattern study leads directly to what we might term "adaptive response."

PERMANENT NEGOTIATION / PERMEABLE BOUNDARIES

"Sensing and awareness" and "pattern study" are important and sensible attributes to possess when approaching megacommunity. But it's easy for leaders to speak of them without actually practicing them. Luckily, these attributes lead to two concepts that provide much less cover. They are much more action-oriented, and much more challenging to the self-protective nature of each sector. In order to activate and sustain optimization, it is necessary to grow comfortable with the concepts of "permanent negotiation" and "permeable boundaries." Receptivity to these concepts is the key to the functioning of a megacommunity in terms of building a workable structure. As such, they are essential elements of the megacommunity mindset.

The definitions of these concepts are plain enough. "Permanent negotiation" defines a state of constant interaction and exchange between the members of the megacommunity. It calls for individuals to recognize the need for constant stakeholder engagement. This steady interchange is an absolute necessity. As a megacommunity forms and progresses, its goals are sure to transform. An attitude of permanent negotiation paves the way for the fluid adjustment of assignments and responsibilities. It will help members navigate what Ruggie points out as the "bumps in the road of an asymmetry that they themselves help to create." And it will help the sectors achieve balance, not in terms of equilibrium per se, but in terms of proactive dynamic tension.

When looking at the optimization of a megacommunity, we found that the term "negotiation" was more appropriate than "collaboration." Collaboration may be a trait associated with megacommunity formation. But negotiation is the key to controlling the operations of a megacommunity once it is past the point of initial convergence. In the legal sphere, negotiation is the process whereby interested parties resolve disputes, agree upon courses of action, bargain for individual or collective advantage, and/or attempt to craft outcomes that serve their mutual interests. All of these points apply within a megacommunity setting.

The concept of "permeable boundaries" calls for megacommunity members to readjust their functioning at the points where they meet, and to allow for more points where they can meet. The concept of "good fences make good neighbors" may apply to megacommunities, when fences are used to delineate the property and responsibilities of any single organization or sector. But it should not be used as a license to create barriers.

In many ways, the megacommunity itself fosters the creation of permeable boundaries. One of the changes that naturally takes place within a megacommunity is the lifting of the artificial blinders that ordinarily keep a leader from looking at the other sectors. Megacommunity boundaries are blurred as the impact of the actions taken by each player is immediate and transversal. But blurring the boundaries is not enough. The ability to come and go—and do so with a welcoming air—is important. Movement across previously blocked chasms needs to be enabled and facilitated.

Megacommunities should test and employ new levels of openness. But this does not call for utter transparency regarding the inner workings of any specific organization. Megacommunity thinking does not seek to throw open or tear apart the functioning of any single organization. As we've said before, it does not call for impossible levels of idealism or utopianism. A glass house is never the best idea. But megacommunity members should strive for complete transparency, regarding the aims of the megacommunity, their part in it, and their understanding of the other players in the megacommunity. They must be completely forthcoming about the issues that are at stake for them, for these issues are the ones that will be at the heart of the megacommunity's ongoing negotiations.

As part of this transparency, it's imperative that members of the megacommunity mean what they say. Consider this example from John

Ruggie: "I remember hearing the story of how [a global beverage company] screwed up with their first promise to support AIDS treatment in Africa. ACT UP and others had put pressure on them to treat their workers in Africa. And after a lot of to-ing and fro-ing, they agreed. And the announcement went out and the NGOs applauded. And then the reality sank in. The company agreed that they would treat their workers. But their workers meant corporate employees, not bottlers, right? A relatively small number. When the reality sank in, they were really beaten up. They were beaten to a pulp . . . Don't promise things you don't mean. And follow through on your commitments."

In other words, megacommunities must build on a foundation of trust.

Permanent negotiation and permeable boundaries are also key to developing a more supple form of recalibration, which is crucial to the megacommunity. An openness to recalibration is a constant in diplomacy, and it is also one of the distinguishing features of sustainable globalization. Consider how it functions even in so seemingly intransigent a giant as China.

"It is fascinating to watch China over time," says Ruggie, "how they have to keep moving in order to recalibrate and re-equilibrate as they go along. 'Yes,' they'll say, 'Come in and pay people in the Pearl River Delta eighty cents an hour and we'll look the other way about pollution and gradually ratchet up.' And now, for the first time, the Chinese have imposed fuel-efficiency standards. And they're comparable to the average Western fuel-efficiency standard. Fifty years ago this would have been unthinkable. The trade-off they face is: 'Look, it's a fact that our labor is cheaper and our regulatory framework less onerous and that will attract investment. At the same time, we don't want to stay there forever. It's not sustainable.'"

A megacommunity takes "recalibration" as a floating factor in globalization and harnesses its power. It can bring a spirit of constant recalibration to unlocking seemingly intractable conflicts between sectors, such as the one Starbucks experienced in Ethiopia, where the coffee company's refusal to recognize Ethiopia's legal ownership of its fine coffee names is eating away at its previous good standing. It aligns with the megacommunity's need for adaptability, its pursuit of best practices and balanced solutions. And it contributes to a megacommunity's scalability—that is, its ability to shrink and grow as needed.

PULLING IT ALL TOGETHER

Optimization. Sensing and awareness. Permanent negotiation. Permeable boundaries. Constant recalibration. All these concepts lead to a profound recognition of interdependence by creating joined capabilities to tackle our toughest problems. These attitudes provide legitimacy to the megacommunity and allow the constituency to align, recognizing the megacommunity as the correct forum in which to kick off a dialogue to harmoniously pursue their interest.

Meanwhile, all these concepts can only help in handling how controversial the megacommunity idea might be in the near future, as it starts to be known. After all, it's an idea that demands change. And, from a more pessimistic angle, it confronts the limits or, worse, the failures of traditional approaches in working out the implications of globalization. From this perspective, it is a harsh critique to leaders who have failed to achieve their mission. However, this is the price of any structural change that implies the natural decline of one set of dynamics and the emergence of a new one.

All these tenets of megacommunity thinking will lead to better understanding and successful action. And with better understanding on all sides, better decisions will be made—which puts us exactly where we need to be to begin the work of megacommunity formation.

CHAPTER FOUR

INITIATING A MEGACOMMUNITY

For Barbara Waugh, head of the Hewlett-Packard Company's University Relations team, improving engineering education in Africa is a matter of the fiercest personal passion. In her book *The Soul in the Computer: The Story of a Corporate Revolutionary,* Waugh writes eloquently about her experience raising two African American children adopted at birth, while chronicling her commitment to corporate change and civil rights. In the mid-2000s, her commitment deepened suddenly and profoundly when her daughter's boyfriend, the father of their unborn son, was murdered. Soon afterward, Waugh made the shocking discovery that while he'd been preparing for his new family, her daughter's boyfriend had also been planning his own funeral. She learned that funeral plans are a fact of life for many young African Americans in inner cities. (In some of these cities, HIV/AIDS infection rates surpass those of some sub-Saharan countries.) Shaken to the core, Waugh vowed to tackle apartheid by race, class, and gender with renewed focus.

"I consciously made this commitment," she says, "for several reasons at once—to save my own soul; to help diminish the tragedies that afflict many individuals, families, and communities in emerging economies, including that of African Americans in the United States; and to help make participation in the global knowledge economy more widespread and robust. I also knew that only those countries that overcome apartheid could compete in the global economy. I hoped to contribute in Africa by working to improve engineering education there." Waugh aspired to mirror the success of another HP team that had done much the same thing in Latin America.

But despite her passion, her 25 years at HP, and HP's commitment to regional economic development, Waugh did not know where to start. Improving education, even in your own country, is an incredibly complex problem. Plus, she had never been to Africa. She went looking for support within HP, but her idea was often greeted with the somewhat deflating response, "Why Africa?" She stepped back, to more carefully consider those who might serve as internal stakeholders in her plan. That's when she decided to call Olivier Suinat, the general manager of HP Africa. There, she found the kind of ignition she'd been looking for.

As Waugh says, Suinat "expressed great enthusiasm for anything we could do to increase the number of engineers in the region. He told me that, as a customer base, Africa was on par with many European markets. Africa is, in fact, one of the fastest-growing emerging market regions in HP's 'Europe, Middle East, and Africa' geography. The general ignorance of this fact within HP astonished me; how could we not know? Were we so blinded by the negative press on Africa—negative stories outnumbered positive stories by a 12-to-1 ratio, according to one research report—that we couldn't even see our own company's success?"

Suinat connected her with HP's new general manager for West Africa, Lloyd Atabansi, with whom she had immediate rapport. ("My first appointment with Lloyd . . . scheduled for one hour . . . expanded to six.") Together, they began to envision a new initiative they dubbed "Engineering Africa."

Waugh realized that she was looking at a problem that could only be successfully addressed by a large, ongoing joint initiative involving many organizations. With Atabansi's input, she decided to put her muscle into continuing to identify stakeholders in Africa.

One key stakeholder emerged from her own University Relations team. Arnaud Pierson, an HP engineer working with UNESCO (United Nations Education, Scientific and Cultural Organization), had developed a capacity-building initiative in southeastern Europe called Brain Gain. According to Waugh, "Universities in the region had lost as much as 80 percent of their faculty and students through attrition during the civil wars in the Balkan states. By equipping key universities in the region with high-end networking equipment, and money for research and exchange travel, these universities upgraded their research, increased enrollment and retention, and joined the global university research community. I asked Arnaud if we could expand the project to Africa. Conversations with UNESCO and the HP philanthropic organization were already under way. The UNESCO team selected Algeria, Nigeria, Ghana, Senegal, Kenya, and Zimbabwe to receive grants. Education ministers in these countries [selected] key universities to participate in the African Brain Gain initiative. Various people involved in that initiative joined the leadership of Engineering Africa."

Momentum accelerated when Russ Jones, chair of the Capacity Building Committee of World Federation of Engineering Organizations (WFEO), decided to join Waugh's efforts. He suggested that HP and WFEO collaborate, and lead together with WFEO as the effort's public face. This approach offered several advantages. First, it was easier for other companies to join an effort not labeled "HP." Second, as in the rest of the world, Africa's engineering academics prefer to join an effort championed by engineering educators and professionals over one driven by corporations, no matter how well intentioned those companies may be. Finally, WFEO already included representatives from 90 countries, including many in Africa.

Now, Waugh had the makings of an effective core team. It was time to expand their outreach dramatically. Jones set out to convene a meeting, which was held in Abuja, Nigeria, in March 2007. Through his many networks, Jones invited cosponsors, including the Nigerian Society of Engineers, the African Engineering Education Association, and the UNESCO

Regional Bureau for Science and Technology in Africa, as well as key faculty in Nigeria and throughout the continent. HP invited companies based in Nigeria, in Africa and globally, as well as Nigerian government ministers. The 50 invited participants included members from all three sectors: engineering educators, industry leaders, government officials, and executives of related nongovernmental organizations, including the World Bank and several local foundations.

"In planning our first conference," says Waugh, "we drew together a core group with the momentum to survive the loss of any one member. That core is already growing, as conference participants discover their passion for this endeavor."

While successful, and unprecedented in its way, the conference was only one of the major building blocks on which Waugh focused. "Even before the spring 2007 Nigerian conference," she adds, "we had laid the groundwork for meetings with the new Nigerian government. We also conceived of a larger conference on the issues facing women in information and communication technologies (ICT) and engineering, to occur later in 2007 at the time of the annual meeting of the Nigerian Society of Engineers, which draws 4,000 people from throughout the country. And we began talking with representatives from other countries who were interested in holding similar workshops."

Although Engineering Africa's efforts are still in the early stages, it has already begun to generate real value. Among other things, says Waugh, they have "discovered that we already have critical resources, concepts, and tools in place for regional economic development through quality assurance in engineering education. And as we identified internal stakeholders in HP, we helped articulate and consolidate a more robust company strategy for Africa."

Waugh and her partners are building such a solid foundation of stakeholders with such a wide variety of influence and capabilities, it's easy to imagine that their efforts will lead to more and more victories in the future. But Waugh can already count one major success in Africa: She identified a problem for which a multi-organizational, multi-sector approach was the only solution—and she has convinced other key stakeholders to commit time and resources to that effort. In other words, she has successfully initiated a megacommunity.

We know what elements define a megacommunity. But having all the elements in place does not mean that a megacommunity will come together on its own. A process of initiation is essential, as Waugh's story demonstrates. A series of conscious actions must be taken.

To be sure, the initiation of any particular megacommunity will not necessarily reflect that of another, in exact detail. The warp and woof of interdependencies within a megacommunity will be as distinctive as those in any community. And yet there are similarities among all megacommunity efforts that suggest a series of universal principles exist, applicable to all. From our direct experience and from extant examples of megacommunity-like actions, we perceive a sequence of goals that can be applied in most circumstances, as well as certain productive variations. Together, they provide a base of procedural steps that are consistent, but also diverse enough to cover the range of megacommunity situations.

THE INITIATORS

A megacommunity might already exist—in a latent state—as a result of the presence of an overlapping set of issues. Most likely, this latent megacommunity will have reached a threshold at which the value of cross-sector action is evident. But the megacommunity will not move from latent to active on its own. While the potential energy is there, the creation of a megacommunity requires a catalyst to convert the potential energy into action. Allowing for the fact that in a moment of crisis—such as a natural disaster—a megacommunity might spontaneously emerge, in most cases, an initiator, or group of initiators, will have to step forward.

An initiator is not a codeword for megacommunity CEO. Nor is it a role that necessarily continues once the megacommunity is established. But it is the most visible leadership role in a megacommunity's embryonic stages. The development of an active megacommunity requires a conscious infusion of energy—and the initiators will be the catalyst for that energy. Once catalyzed, a channel will be created whereby other stakeholders can add their energy and resources. In this regard, the question "How does a megacommunity form?" may be more rightly asked as: "How can I contribute to the formation of a megacommunity?"

1) BUSINESS SECTOR INITIATORS

Initiators may arise from any sector depending on the specific situation, although we suspect that many of them will have business-sector experience. The business sector is in a better position than either government or civil society to absorb the risk largely because it, collectively, has more resources (in terms of funds and people). Take for example another Hewlett-Packard initiative: the work of HP's University Relations (UR) team in Latin America. In 2002, recognizing the global dearth of software engineers, a group of five Hewlett-Packard staff members used their resources to start a megacommunity-based approach to developing and recruiting technical talent. They were able to dedicate a large amount of time to this project, focusing on research, outreach, and the convening of conferences around the world. It helped that they had already established UR as a unit of HP Labs, which was already engaged with over 100 academic institutions. (As we've seen time and again, the involvement of university-based research proves to be an incredibly important component in forming a megacommunity enterprise.) They drew in local government education bureaus, the World Federation of Engineering Organizations, and representatives in Latin America from the Organization of American States.

With people from all these institutions regularly meeting, Hewlett-Packard was able to establish collaborative research programs and broaden funding, as well as build the HP brand and aid in recruitment. Barbara Waugh, whose efforts in Africa echo HP's work in Latin America, describes the logic behind the initiative this way:

"World-class engineering education, developed with industry partnership, doesn't just provide workers in the short term for the jobs that industry has. It also attracts further investment that in turn helps the region or country retain its graduates, rather than lose them to emigration."

In essence, Hewlett-Packard's UR group initiated a megacommunity, without actually calling it a megacommunity—although HP is using the term to describe its subsequent "capacity building" in Africa. HP's efforts in Africa and Latin America prove how useful the business sector can be in getting a megacommunity off the ground.

2) CIVIL SECTOR INITIATORS

Though businesses may find it easier at times, NGOs and government agencies can also take the initiator role in a megacommunity. NGO leaders may indeed find themselves cast in the initiator role when it comes to megacommunities that form around social and environmental issues, issues that tend to stem from a culture of altruism and are fueled by personal passion. We see that happening around issues such as HIV/AIDS and, more recently, global climate change. But NGOs can also play a key role in megacommunity-like actions that form around fair-business practices.

For example, the International Oxfam network—a confederation of nationally affiliated nonprofits with different priorities—and Starbucks initially formed a relationship in 2002 when Oxfam Great Britain approached leading coffee-buying companies about its planned sustainable coffee campaign. Although aspects of this partnership ran aground due to concerns over trademark practices—a problem that might have been overcome with better megacommunity facilitation—there is no doubt that Oxfam's initial outreach to Starbucks was in effect an effort to seed a megacommunity.

Oxfam GB initially decided Starbucks would be a good collaborator on the issue because Starbucks had already developed long-term contracts with some producers, expanding its Fair Trade purchases (even though that only accounts for a very small percentage of all coffee it buys). Plus Starbucks had already instituted purchasing guidelines that stipulated a series of social and environmental standards farmers must meet in return for better terms.

The farming cooperatives in Ethiopia were aware of their role in this relationship, and the Ethiopian government recognized its opportunity to optimize coffee production through the Oxfam-Starbucks relationship in its country. Head of Corporate Social Responsibility and Communications, Scott Keiller, Starbucks UK, explained the agreement was "a mutual realization that by working together we could achieve more than by working alone."

The success of the venture was measured by Oxfam via baselining socioeconomic surveys, including factors such as the level of women's literacy and the amount of irrigated land, underscoring the fact that Oxfam clearly recognized the connection between fair business practices and its mission to work with others to overcome poverty and suffering, marking it as a valid initiator.

3) GOVERNMENT SECTOR INITIATORS

Those from the government sector can also find themselves in the initiator role. Although the government sector traditionally has less fiscal discretion, and is often mired in political constraints, the government may find itself in an initiator role when top political figures pick up issues as "pet projects," or a particular amount of funding is set aside for a specific issue, or when an issue is simply too huge to be handled by any other entity.

That's exactly what happened in Florida in the wake of Hurricane Andrew. It was Florida's local government response agencies that drew together a group of national and local government leaders, nonprofit groups, and Florida-based corporations—including insurance and logistics companies. In turn, that group developed a rapid response approach for future natural disasters. The megacommunity, in short, is credited with Florida's subsequent success in mobilizing a response to tropical storms, a marked contrast to the failures in response to Hurricane Katrina. The Andrew aftermath shows that there are times when the government may be the only one who can step forward to play the initiator role; and the Katrina aftermath shows the deadly consequences that sometimes result when government officials don't step forward.

INTERNAL ANALYSIS

If you suspect that a megacommunity might be useful, and see the outline of a latent megacommunity appearing around your organization or around an issue salient to your organization, that certainly puts you on the path toward initiation. But the first question to ask is whether you are the best person/organization to successfully convene the megacommunity. In many cases, you will have a strong intuitive sense that indeed you are. But in some cases, a certain amount of internal analysis may be necessary. The following list of attributes and conditions go a long way toward defining the best possible initiators.

1) Initiators must be clear on their own vital interests. This may seem like an incredibly rudimentary idea, but it is surprising how many organizations do not have a clear idea where their full set of vital interests lay.

Consider what happened to the Coca-Cola Company when it opened a bottling plant in Kerala, India, just as the region entered a three-year cycle of moderate-to-severe drought. In 2003, BBC Radio aired a report claiming that the testing of bio-solids from that Coca-Cola plant indicated that their products contained unsafe levels of cadmium and lead.[1] Then, in 2004, activists claimed that the Coca-Cola bottling plant in Kerala was depleting the aquifer by unreasonably withdrawing groundwater. Finally, amid local and international protest and ongoing legal and regulatory disputes, Coca-Cola decided to close the plant.[2]

While Coca-Cola had a business interest in operating the plant, what became clear to its leadership is that water—not just its availability, but its plenitude, and the ability of a company to be a provider and replenisher of water—turned out to be one of the company's vital interests. And more importantly, they didn't realize this vital interest was shared with a large number of stakeholders—whom we refer to as the latent megacommunity. Ultimately, Coca-Cola's membership in the latent water-scarcity megacommunity could no longer be ignored. For the record, since that time, the Coca-Cola Company launched the Environment and Water Resources department, completed 864 plant-level water risk assessments worldwide, and has also begun to develop a company-wide water strategy.

As the Kerala example shows, vital interests are not always self-evident. It also shows that waiting for someone outside your organization to pressure you into realizing your vital interest is not the best thing for your organization. Instead, some form of thorough "self analysis" is called for.

What does the "self analysis" entail? Obviously, it depends on the organization and the issues to a great extent, but generally the following points should be considered:

- What are the major drivers of value, impact, or earnings for your organization?
- Upon whom do you depend for the major drivers of value, impact, or earnings for your organization (that is, what is your extended enterprise)?
- What do you consider to be the strategic risks to your organization?
- Which global issues have a direct and material impact on your organization? And which have an indirect impact?
- What issues are your colleagues / peers concerned about?
- What issues are your partners / suppliers concerned about?

These questions are just a starting point. This evolution will often require some forecasting along the lines of strategic risk management. Ultimately, initiators need to identify and understand the long-range factors that stand in the way of achieving an organization's goals, or the ways in which one's sense and/or definition of "vital interest" needs to evolve.

2) Initiators should see the greatest value in convening a megacommunity over any other approach to a solution. What this means, simply and directly, is that the best initiators will be those who are the most motivated. This motivation may arise from the fact that they feel the most pain, financially or emotionally (allowing that those in certain sectors might act from altruistic impulses). Or it may arise from the fact that they foresee the fullest range of gain. For example, in its work developing software engineers in Latin America, Hewlett-Packard not only recognized the economic needs of the countries involved, it clearly saw its own need for new recruits and markets, as well as an intensification of brand identification, proliferation, and reputation.

This motivation may arise from the fact that in identifying and forecasting their vital interests, an organization has come to clearly understand that it requires ties to other organizations and sectors. But there are many other ways an organization may come to the keen (and sometimes painful) conclusion that there are certain problems that can't be solved within their own walls. They may have gotten burned (as in the case of Coca-Cola in Kerala, or Enel SpA in Brindisi) or they may be experiencing, as sometimes happens in the paradigm-shifting context of globalization, the sudden dawning of enlightened leadership. Whatever the case, good initiators should be among those who have a deep need for the megacommunity.

3) Initiators should have standing, a pre-existing reputation and relation-ships that can help get the megacommunity off the ground. In network analysis, a hub is a node with a high number of linkages. And while every initiator does not have to be a hub, it is important for the initia-tors to have some important pre-existing relationships. In the best case scenario, relationships that exist in advance of megacommunity forma-tion may provide the best initial foundation for cooperation. Reaching out only when a problem arises can create mistrust, distrust, and suspi-cion. Hence, the importance of building network capital, as we dis-cussed in chapter three.

In an organization that values network capital, people will already possess some understanding of their colleagues' interests, capabilities, and agenda. In fact, the best way to ensure that you are not co-opting others' agenda is to understand their agenda. Over time, this level of understand-ing will come from continued exposure to other organizations and sec-tors within the megacommunity. But during a megacommunity's early stages, awareness must come from cultivating your network, and learning more about the ways in which your colleagues from other organizations, in each of their own spheres, drive to commitment and to action.

Again, this is another reason why organizations that function as hubs may make the best initiators. A hub not only has many connections with many other bodies, but by its very nature, it is connected on many different levels. The same hub organization might connect with others as a supplier, a customer, a "regulatee," an icon, or a competitor, an adver-sary, or in any number of other ways. The various natures of these con-nections only add to a hub's standing in a potential megacommunity.

4) Initiators should come from organizations that value innovation. Good initiators are comfortable with the idea of using inductive reasoning to project a future payoff. They are willing to take an informed leap of faith. They do not need to know that something has been done successfully a hundred times before.

Consider the challenge of selling the first telephone in a system. The second person buying a phone knows he has someone to talk to, but the first purchaser has to believe in the future value of the system. The salesperson selling the second, third, and fourth telephone can point to the actual value of the network in a sales pitch. But trying to sell that first phone requires a leap of faith.

Secondarily, the more organizations structure innovative thinking into their decision-making, the stronger—and more dependable—initiators they will be. This is where the business sector may have a slight advantage, since megacommunity initiation can be seen as an extension of the day-to-day business mindset of finding new solutions to market approaches. To be sure, NGOs and governments have shown themselves capable of developing ingenious and innovative approaches. But the business sector will have the most experience in this regard. They are accustomed to doing market research, building business models, and preparing for market-oriented risks—and they have the resources in place to back it up.

5) Initiators should undertake some degree of organizational analysis before reaching out. To initiate a megacommunity requires a commitment—and therefore, as in any business or policy decision, an initiator must be prepared to decide how best to organize and use their resources and how to prepare their organization for this new investment.

A structured process may be required, but there is no need to over-mystify this process. It is what companies do, in most cases, every day. As our colleague Daniel Lewis, points out, "There's a rule for every major corporation that it's not enough to recognize the constraints you're operating under. Rather, you have to be part of groups that apply pressure on things that need to change. In two steps, you first take in the environment, then develop a strategy for change."

When preparing for megacommunity initiation, "taking in the environment" is a key stage that cannot be overlooked. It breaks down into several internal areas of effort:

INTERNAL DEPARTMENTAL ANALYSIS

Enel SpA, the Italian power company whose plans for a new energy facility in Brindisi had been blocked, conducted a thorough internal analysis after the event. Their team discovered that each department was operating too much as a separate entity. They also uncovered the fact that over time, a single department had garnered enough influence to act as sole leader of operations. The company's leaders set about making changes to these structural imbalances, hoping to improve communication and to pave the way for a megacommunity approach to future projects. Any initiator should make sure that the balance of influence among departments is a healthy one, and that the lines of communication are sufficiently open within their organization, since this will be a model that carries over into the megacommunity.

INTERNAL STAKEHOLDER ANALYSIS

One important internal step is the identification of stakeholders *within* your own corporation. Who in the organization will be most affected by the decision to become part of a megacommunity? Internal stakeholder analysis will provide the first layer of knowledge regarding who in the organization needs to join the megacommunity effort. And it leads directly to one extremely important action: consensus building.

Internal Consensus Building

It is necessary to achieve a high level of visibility and support within your organization—both for yourself and for the idea of megacommunity—before going outside your organization. You must be able to articulate the relevance of forming a megacommunity and the risks of refusing to engage with the outer world. You must be prepared to move your organization toward a willingness to commit its resources both "in" and "out."

In other words, before initiating a megacommunity, you have to get key leaders in your organization to buy into the practical case for operating within a megacommunity. By nature of their internal culture, some organizations might find this a relatively easy task. Here again, it is clear that an organization that recognizes the importance of network capital and values innovation will have an easier time with this task. In other cases, you may find that repositioning steps are needed at the top management level, and that the strategic agenda needs to be shaped in a particular way to follow a megacommunity management approach.

Internal Team Building

After undertaking internal stakeholder analysis, an organization should have a good idea who will be on its megacommunity team. But they also need to figure out how that team might be structured. They need to determine which issues of vital interest need to be managed and by whom. A dedicated staff will be called upon to successfully map out relevant stakeholders, use research (and the analysis of this research) to prioritize them, and then employ tailored engagement mechanisms—steps that take us to the brink of our first external steps.

EXTERNAL ANALYSIS

While assessing your internal situation and beginning to make whatever adjustments and preparations are necessary, an initiator can then start the process of collecting external data. As we've seen in the Hewlett Packard example at the start of this chapter, some level of external analysis should precede any formal attempts to reach outside your own organization if one hopes to convene a healthy megacommunity, with a relevant set of players in place (keeping in mind that once initiated, the healthy megacommunity will continue to grow and evolve, adding new members).

In many ways, external analysis mirrors internal analysis. As such, it once again involves an assessment of stakeholders as a primary function.

In other words: Who should I be reaching out to in my search for mega-community members?

First and foremost, keep in mind that when exploring and analyzing a potential megacommunity, restricting yourself to obvious institutional sources of knowledge is not necessarily the best approach. For example, according to Curt Struble, the former U.S. ambassador to Peru, "Many U.S. companies have come to Latin America to expand their businesses and they talk to a lawyer or to the formal authorities about the requirements. But they're making a mistake. The local authorities are not representing the local people; they simply make decisions for them.

"I've seen many instances when well-intentioned groups or businesses gave standing and validity to marginal players, or radical players, simply by admitting them to the table. You want to make sure that the people who are seen as representing local interest groups are, in fact, valid interlocutors that are in the mainstream."

In other words, it is important to get the right players in the room. You do not want to waste energy by engaging with the wrong set of individuals: those without the power to deliver on a shared commitment, or "false leaders," purposely sent to the table to slow down the process. You also do not want to engage solely with people like yourself, and therefore miss the opportunity to get an accurate view of the priorities of the larger community. To develop reliable insight, Ambassador Struble recommends that "a leader must reach out to a wider cross-section of people" than might be included on a first pass.

There are different ways this search for stakeholders can be defined and conducted, depending on your prior knowledge of the players, the breath of the issue at the megacommunity's center, or the size of the geographic area involved. This search will also be affected by the amount and type of resources at hand.

1) A FULL MAPPING OF STAKEHOLDERS

Some organizations may choose to take Ambassador Struble's "wider cross-section" and expand it to include the *widest* possible cross-section of stakeholders imaginable. Once again, it's the business sector that will likely have the resources available to conduct such an extensive search. For example, Enel SpA, mindful of its Brindisi experience, is using a very different approach in Italy's Veneto region, along the Po River, where it plans to overhaul current power-generating plants to burn green coal. Enel came to the understanding that the Brindisi case was not an isolated episode. It was the result of significant and longstanding concerns on the part of local communities regarding health and safety. In the Veneto region, the power company's leaders have recognized the need to be ahead of this curve and, in honest broker fashion, they are moving into that community with much more sensitivity and hard knowledge.

Members of the power company's strategic planning department, communications, infrastructure and network engineering departments, and the department responsible for institutional relationships have mapped the megacommunity with a matrix that includes an exhaustive list of stakeholders, spells out their interests and objectives, and underscores any special inter-relationships between them. Enel's analysis identified more that 100 stakeholders among central, regional, and local entities.

Enel SpA clustered the various stakeholders into three groups: institutions (political, administrative, academic, social/health services, research); associations (religious, unions, environmental/agriculture, industry/commerce, consumers); and media (TV, radio, newspapers, blogs). Moreover, a level of criticality was assigned to each stakeholder in order to obtain a table of the risks and oppositions categorized by each constituency.

The various tables and charts that follow (see figures 4.1 and 4.2) will aid Enel SpA as a decision support tool. It helps Enel discover the region's areas of potential instability and opportunity, anticipate the impact of its possible actions in the Veneto, and modulate its actions accordingly, for its own benefit and the benefit of the entire megacommunity.

Members of the power company's strategic planning department, communications department, and a department responsible for institutional relationships also mapped the megacommunity within a matrix that shows the interrelationships of all key players, and that will help the company discover the region's areas of potential instability and opportunity, and anticipate the impact of its possible actions in Veneto.

Mapping Across Borders

In conducting a complete stakeholder analysis, it is also wise to assess the kinds of economic/political/social environments into which the megacommunity in question may be moving. As discussed in chapter three, a particular megacommunity may involve constituencies in different parts of the globe. And in many ways, the goals of that megacommunity will be a function of geography. Democracies may provide the

FIGURE 4.1: THE MEGACOMMUNITY MATRIX

PARAMETER		VENETO	ITALY	DESCRIPTION
PRIVATE SECTOR				
Real GDP growth	2005	0.3%	0.2%	GDP growth of Veneto is aligned with national levels after three years of lower growth
	2006	1.5%	1.5%	
	2007	1.6%	1.5%	
Employment composition 2004	Agriculture	4%	4%	Employment in the industrial sector in Veneto is higher than in the rest of Italy; however, this sector is decreasing, mostly because of challenges faced by mechanical and textile companies
	Industry	39%	29%	
	Service	57%	67%	
Gini index (measures income inequality) 2003		0.294	0.321	Veneto shows a more uniform distribution of income than does the nation (the higher the Gini, the more unequal the distribution of income)
PRIVATE SECTOR				
Salary increases 2004		3.2%	2.9%	The average salary increase in the Veneto region has been higher than national levels
Growth in number of companies 2004		0.6%	1.6%	Companies in Veneto have been challenged; growth rate of active companies has been higher in Italy as a whole than in Veneto
Energy deficit 2004		19.2%	14.0%	During 2003-2004, the regional energy deficit had a significant increase, becoming worse than the Italian one (during 2002, Veneto had a surplus); deficit was due mainly to a reduction of produced energy
PUBLIC SECTOR				
Average tenure of elected government	Historic	2.5 yrs.	1.6 yrs.	Since 1995, there has been a healthy stability of regional/local governments (compared to national levels)
	Recent	5 yrs.	5 yrs.	
Human capital recruitment mechanism		n.a.	n.a.	Data on consideration by talented university graduates of politics as a viable career opportunity, was unavailable
CIVIL SOCIETY				
Volunteers 2001-03		+2.1%	+1.9%	Volunteer rate in Veneto is higher than the rest of Italy
Associations per 10,000 inhabitants 2003		4.3	3.6	Level of associations was higher in Veneto than in the rest of Italy
Average life span		80.7 yrs.	79.9 yrs.	The average lifespan in Veneto is higher than that of the national level

This is a simplified and abridged version of a matrix diagram being used by the Italian utility company Enel to gain awareness of the potential megacommunity in the Veneto region. This table shows the interrelationships of all key players. Section 1 presents a picture of the salient economy of the region. Section 2 assesses local corporations, showcasing the potential for economic development. Section 3

(continues)

FIGURE 4.1 (CONTINUED)

examines the characteristics of local government, while Section 4 charts the outline of the area's civil society, including active NGOs and their financing mechanisms. A weight is assigned to each element, and that helps determine which constituents are needed to join the conversation.

Source: Booz Allen Hamilton and Enel SpA

most robust environment for megacommunities, but megacommunities should not—and cannot—be limited to mature democracies. "You have to decide based on the objective conditions of the countries you're in," says former President Bill Clinton. "For example, if you operate in one of the former Soviet republics, you've got the fastest growing rates of AIDS in the world. But you've got a well-educated workforce. So you can get in there and stomp it in a hurry. If you want to branch into a non-rich Middle Eastern country, there's almost no AIDS, but there are low levels of useful education and sustainable economic enterprise. So you need to figure out how to create better educated, more well-heeled consumers. In other words, the facts will differ in different countries and regions."

As Clinton suggests, you will be confronted by different sets of possibilities depending on where your megacommunity hopes to perform. You will also be confronted by different balances of power and influence among the three sectors, as well as different types of power structures, such as tribal groups. Among other things, it is essential to keep your eye on such profound differences as the maturation of private sector, religious beliefs, attitudes toward natural resource utilization ("Do we preserve or cut down the rainforest?"), presence of a middle class, position of the "rule of law," and the state of a nation's NGO structure. All of

FIGURE 4.2: MAPPING THE MEGACOMMUNITY—

CONSTITUENTS AND CONSENSUS

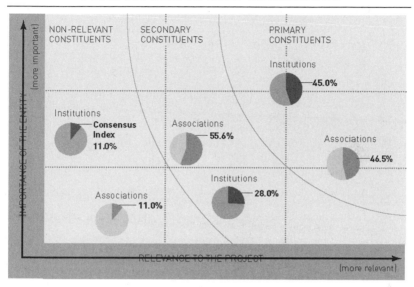

This figure demonstrates how to visually represent stakeholders' positions on a given issue. It is a subjective assessment from the point of view of an initiator. Like most visualizations, there is a lot of information packed into the field of view. There are three bands of constituents (non-relevant, secondary, and primary) to help the initiator understand who they should focus efforts on. Next, the constituents in this example are divided into two groups (associations and institutions) and each group is placed on a grid based on their general standing (importance) and their relevance to the issue. For each group, there is also an assessment of the degree of convergence within that group. This is done using two tailored measures: The consensus index and the index quality. The consensus index measures the orientation (from favorable to contrary) of the constituents related to the major infrastructure project. It provides insights on the level of turbulence / social risk around the project. The index quality measures the reliability of the consensus index—i.e., the percentage of the constituents within the segment for which the orientation is known.

Source: Booz Allen Hamilton and Enel SpA

these differences will affect your approach and level of expectations in terms of your vital interests.

Using "Open Source" Analysis

This type of external stakeholder analysis is, in large part, a harvesting activity. It works from the good assumption that the more research and analysis you do, the more rock solid your first foundation steps will be. An astounding amount of information is available through "open source" analysis, that is, the use of sources that are publicly available and not gathered through any clandestine or illegal methods. Hewlett-Packard, for example, found that plugging into the vast array of university-based research proved incredibly helpful in its work in Latin America.

In many cases, businesses already conduct this kind of research. Consider a company like Mitsubishi. According to author Larry Kahaner, in his book *Competitive Intelligence,* the company "has about thirteen thousand employees in more than two hundred offices worldwide. They collect more than thirty thousand pieces of business and competitive information *daily.* This data is filtered, analyzed, and disseminated to companies within the Mitsubishi family to be used as ammunition in the ongoing global war against competitors."[3] In the megacommunity framework, this information would be used less as ammunition and more as a shared field of data employed to direct megacommunity development and operations.

Open source information can be retrieved by monitoring news services and other data sources (such as trade publications) or you can outsource the collection and synthesis of this information to the many third-party business intelligence companies that have proliferated in the information age. And, of course, the Internet is a primary source for thorough, consistently updated information. Using a simple "key word" search of the Web will point to many players involved in whatever issue you're investigating, such as, say, the preservation of old-growth forests. A key word search will identify the organizations that mention old-growth forests on their Web site, and how interconnected their site is to other sites. The amount of connections to any specific site is an indicator of importance. Developing a talent for open-source analysis can be very useful in helping an initiator identify stakeholders that may not at first be apparent, those without whom you have a natural or obvious connection, or those whose importance is obscured by too many degrees of separation.

Avoiding Thinking-Traps

When conducting a full mapping of stakeholders, there are a few thinking traps that are easy to fall into. They lead to a few basic rules of thumb, some of which may appear counterintuitive at first.

Never freeze your stakeholder map: No matter how thorough a first mapping has been, it is just that: a first mapping. Stakeholders will change over time. A healthy megacommunity is adaptable, growing and shrinking as its goals warrant. By the very nature of problem solving, collaboration, and life, new stakeholders will always be arriving on the scene, while others will leave. Prepare to keep your map fluid.

Do not exclude the opposition: Although this should be obvious by now, it's imperative to keep in mind that when identifying groups with an "overlap in vital interests," you do not eliminate those whose inter-ests may seem opposed to your most immediate interests. You must rec-ognize that those in projected opposition might—and, in most cases, *will*—know something you don't.

For example, the companies and governments that made up the Fourth International Conference on Avian Influenza in 2006 called for an immediate culling of infected wild birds. But Birdlife International, a global bird conservation group that possessed salient information, did not have a seat at the conference. It might have been thought that "bird conservation" was not a relevant, and possibly oppositional, viewpoint. And, in fact, Birdlife International did indeed have an anticulling stance. But that stance was not based on rhetoric, or on some avian form of political correctness. It was based on a study that had already shown that culling can cause the virus to spread more quickly, by chas-ing surviving carriers to new places, and causing the previously healthy bird population to become stressed and therefore more prone to infec-tion.[4] That information should have been included—and certainly would have been helpful—in any conference organized to arrest the spread of avian flu.

A megacommunity's all-inclusive attitude is very different from the one at play in the example above. In a megacommunity, it is wise to ulti-mately connect to as many players in the megacommunity's interest-zone as possible. Hence, our next rule of thumb.

The megacommunity must develop "weak ties": As we briefly men-tioned in chapter two, the concept of weak ties was introduced by Stan-ford University Professor Mark Granovetter. In his paper entitled "The

Strength of Weak Ties."[5] Granovetter documented a study of two groups in Boston that were working to stem the flood of 1970s-era "urban development." He looked at the approaches taken by both groups and concluded that the more effective group was the one that included the presence of "weak ties"—connections between participants who did not know each other that well or have all that much in common.

The basic idea argues that weak ties in a social network (like a megacommunity) are as important as the strong ties (connections of like-minded players in your supply network or, on a larger scale, your sector). A group that includes weak ties receives insights, news, or other important information earlier than those with only strong ties. And experience shows that they are able to more quickly organize themselves to take action. (See figure 4.3)

Granovetter's argument is this: Strong ties are transitive (meaning that if a given relation exists between "a" and "b" and between "b" and "c," then it also exists between "a" and "c."). So, if two individuals have a common close friend, then it is likely that they are related—as in, "friend of my friend is also my friend." Strong ties pervade densely packed networks. But while weak ties are much less transitive, they cover a larger area. Weak ties are more likely to be bridges—connecting different subgroups (or cliques) in the social network of the megacommunity.

In many cases, the information obtained through a strong tie is likely to be very similar to the information a participant already has. On the other hand, weak ties are more likely to open up information sources very different from one's own.

FIGURE 4.3: WEAK TIES WITHIN A NETWORK

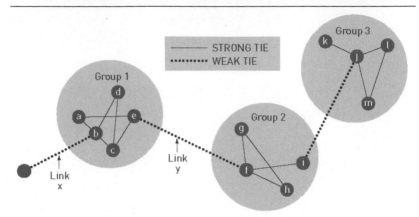

The figure illustrates Granovetter's thoughts regarding the role weak ties play in a network. The large colored circles represent groups with strong obvious ties. Strong ties pervade groups. Link X represents a weak tie in the form of an individual entity that connects to only one member of the megacommunity, but might be very useful to the megacommunity. Link Y shows another type of weak tie: two groups that are connected due to a single relationship between individual members of each group. This figure shows that weak ties can help a megacommunity cover a larger area than that of a megacommunity made up of strong ties alone.

Source: Booz Allen Hamilton

In order to form or activate a megacommunity, leaders must utilize weak ties to reach out beyond their sector, beyond their geographical location, and access the latent connections of the networked world. Without weak-tie connections, the megacommunity will not grow appropriately, information will not spread, relationships will not build, and a diversity of opinions will not be incorporated. Weak ties also bring in much needed specialized capabilities often overlooked at first. In many ways, harnessing the power of weak ties is one of the main benefits of operating within a megacommunity.

2) A TIERED APPROACH TO STAKEHOLDER ANALYSIS

Reaching out to weak ties and oppositional players is certainly part of Enel's approach to stakeholder gathering. It's the most thorough one we've seen. But there are other approaches that can work in the first phase of megacommunity formation. In one of the Hewlett-Packard examples we've previously cited, HP's University Relations team in Latin America began with a core group of like-minded thinkers they'd identified in Brazil. Then, over time, they reached out to more stakeholders—and with great success. According to Barbara Waugh, "In nine years, grassroots conversations and projects led by Lueny Morell, HP's University Relations director for Latin America, and by Russ Jones, chair of the Capacity Building Committee of WFEO, scaled up to involve multiple stakeholders from industry, universities, and governmental and non-governmental agencies (such as engineering education and accreditation agencies)." Today, this network has grown to include "the Organization of American States Ministers of Science and Technology, funding bodies such as the Inter-American Development Bank and the World Bank, and various organizations that support programs for the innovation of engineering education and the establishment of quality assurance mechanisms in the region."

In a case like this, stakeholder analysis and first contact happen concurrently. Core stakeholders can be identified and asked to join the process of initiation. Core stakeholders may be ones with whom you already have a relationship. They may be ones of which you share intimate, in-depth knowledge, who you know to have a previous commitment to action and actionable results, who you know are willing to dialogue and engage. In some cases, they might be organizations whose goals are very close to your own. In others, they might be organizations who you know will bring a different and much-needed perspective from the onset.

Of course, when using a tiered or phased approach to stakeholder analysis and development, the most efficient thing you can do is attempt to identify a hub. Just as Oxfam did when it partnered with Starbucks, an initiator might find itself reaching out to an organization big enough, powerful enough, smart enough, and connected enough to serve as a hub. The earliest stakeholder analysis—as well as previous knowledge of a particular landscape—should result in the identification of hubs.

By their nature, hubs will have significantly more connections than the average node. Therefore, in a phase-one megacommunity, the function of the hub would be to automatically bring others along and give the initiator access to new resources needed to get vital tasks accomplished. They can also play a key role—by nature of their influence and resources—in setting behavior norms in the community and enforcing agreed upon rules.

Either way, the development of a core constituency or the engagement of a hub can facilitate the growth of the megacommunity, as well as solidifying the megacommunity's base, keeping in mind that as the number of stakeholders increase, the easier it is to add more to the community. Remember: This is a phase-one approach, with the ultimate goal of achieving as robust and inclusive a group of stakeholders as you would using the full-mapping approach.

ACTIVATING THE LATENT MEGACOMMUNITY

Once a core group of initiators is established, it is up to that group to begin activating the latent megacommunity. The first order of business is to articulate an answer to John Ruggie's question: "What do you converge behind?" Ruggie's question, which goes to the heart of megacommunity functioning at every stage, is especially challenging in the earliest stages. The challenge is reduced somewhat when the core group of initiators is very clear about the focus of the megacommunity—the overlapping vital interest.

The development of a clear, complete, and compelling statement capturing the overlapping vital interest goes directly to the heart of the megacommunity's inherent value in recognizing, responding, and acting with an eye toward the connections between local and global issues. An important part of the messaging is linking local issues to global trends to propel and steer interest. Global concerns about the climate change, pollution, and greenhouse gases, for example, definitely play a role in forging the conscience of the local population, as they have in both Enel cases we've cited.

In defining the overlapping vital interest, there are a few caveats to keep in mind. Too general a statement—that is, saving the planet—will not be useful. It makes the problem too large and diffuse for the megacommunity to tackle. Although many megacommunity issues are issues of geocomplexity at their highest scale, geocomplexity is a way of thinking about problems at the highest level of abstraction, and can be the least useful approach for revealing convergence, a defining feature of megacommunity.

Think of problems in terms of a waterfall effect. Start at the top with an abstraction of the problem, then deconstruct the abstract problem into more understandable parts, then associate those parts with local concerns. Finding the overlap in issues can help a player define the deconstructed problem in a way that is meaningful to them and understandable by others—which leads directly to the fact that a well-articulated "overlapping vital interest" suggests potential actions that can be taken. After all, the entire megacommunity idea exists as a way of making complex problems more actionable.

Conversely, too narrow a statement can over-restrict the potential for enticing new or other members into the megacommunity. For example, in Enel SpA efforts in the Veneto region, if the overlapping vital interest is defined as solving the problem of carbon emissions, the membership in the megacommunity is limited to the utility, specific watchdog groups, and the government as a regulator. If instead the issue is viewed as the importance of sustainable energy to a region, then more members have a stake. Available, affordable energy drives commerce and GDP growth, gives a local community more appeal, improves quality of life—and in no way ignores the carbon issue.

The overlapping vital interest, if properly defined, should not unduly limit the megacommunity in either composition or scope. It allows the megacommunity to grow and sustain, to be applicable to new and specific challenges. An overlapping vital interest should reflect a viewpoint that transcends the singular perspective that an individual player brings to the megacommunity. As we've suggested, an overlapping vital interest makes the features of convergence all the more real. Convergence is the commitment to mutual action that all members must work toward.

The overlapping vital interest must be allowed to evolve as you engage the latent megacommunity and as its core of constituents grows larger. It will modify itself to reflect the specific concerns of the members, and it might also experience a wholesale scaling-up of goals (much like the Harlem Initiative did when it grew from a Harlem-based plan to one that has now been imported to several cities throughout the United States, escalating from local to regional). A truly successful megacommunity should scale over time. But the way it scales depends on the way its vital interest is understood, described, and conceived at the outset.

Activating the latent megacommunity should address not only issues of engagement but also the process of engagement. Before stakeholders are actively sought, it might be wise to agree upon a process for engagement within the initiating body. And perhaps this process should be published externally, so that potential participants in a megacommunity will have a good idea of how that particular organization plans to interact with them. An initiator needs to be very clear and public about the megacommunity it is hoping to create. Transparency is key. There should be nothing clandestine about a megacommunity. Besides, keeping the public eye on leadership is a way to ensure that relationships follow through.

In many ways, identifying stakeholders, visualizing the shape of the megacommunity, and articulating the overlapping vital interest might be referred to as "pre-forming activities." But in megacommunities, pre-forming and initiation can be overlapping steps, especially if they lead you on a course of first contacts. Once this happens, convergence becomes increasingly apparent. And the critical move toward a working structure officially begins.

CHAPTER 5

STRUCTURING AND SUSTAINING THE MEGACOMMUNITY

L

ike too many great natural resources, Australia's Great Barrier Reef is under attack. The Great Barrier Reef (GBR) is the world's largest coral reef. It stretches over 1,600 miles along the coast of Queensland and supports an incredible diversity of sea life including over 30 species of whales, dolphins, and porpoises. In 1997, CNN dubbed it one the seven natural wonders of the world.[1] But in the past decades, the Reef has experienced an overlapping series of threats from overfishing, runoff (which leads to diminishing water quality), cyclical outbreaks of crown-of-thorns starfish, and perhaps most significantly, the effects of global climate change (which causes the temperature of the Coral Sea to rise and leads to mass coral bleaching). Some have predicted that, for all intents and purposes, the Reef will cease to exist by 2050.

For years, individual scientists and marine science labs inside universities had been tracking these changes, issuing warnings, and proposing solutions. But these efforts were largely uncoordinated, and the problems persisted. According to John Schubert, Chairman of the Commonwealth Bank of Australia and currently chair of the Foundation, "There was limited communication between the various institutions." In other words, those concerned had failed to establish an effective megacommunity. But with the creation of The Great Barrier Reef Foundation, a more coordinated effort soon became apparent.

The Great Barrier Reef Foundation was founded by an independent group of businessmen "to bring the various research organizations together, so that they could build upon each others' work rather than have them compete with each other." However, Schubert realized that in the spirit of megacommunity, the foundation also needed to reach out to a broader array of stakeholders.

One decisive roadblock stood in the way: key players on the Reef needed to agree on the major threats to the Reef's future and needed to identify their overlapping vital interest. According to Schubert, "As we went out to raise money for research from the private sector, we found that we were inhibited in that we couldn't explain well where the particular research project we were trying to get funding for fitted into the overall scheme of things." The foundation also realized that they had to work on "getting an understanding of the current knowledge in relation to those threats, what we need to know in order to manage those threats, and work on closing the gap between what we know and what we need to know."

The government had begun work on its own study of top ranking threats. Ironically, in a demonstration of a megacommunity's network facility, the government commissioned this study from a marine and tropical research facility they had put together whose chief executive turned out to be the chairman of the megacommunity's scientific advisory committee. The government and the megacommunity's overall characterization of the threats soon aligned, and the nature of the overlapping vital interest was identified.

A plan of action could then be put in place. Now the megacommunity could define a set of goals, a common language, and a working structure.

One important aspect of the structure of this particular megacommunity concerns the raising of funds. According to Schubert, the structure of the Reef megacommunity is very much along the lines of a "business approach, with the science somewhat running in parallel or a bit ahead. While a new strategic plan was being developed by the key Reef agencies, we were going to go to business groups we knew. That's where we were going to try and get the funding. We wanted to strengthen the board. We started to form a new group—the Chairman's Panel."

As developed, the megacommunity's Chairman's Panel invites the chief executives of the top 50 companies in Australia to help the foundation fund the future of the GBR. "They pay $15,000 a year for a three-year appointment," says Schubert, "and they get to come to one of the islands which have a research station on it and spend a couple of days with the foundation's elite faculty of scientists, snorkeling and learning about the Reef in science workshops and also commenting on the foundation's business plan. We also get them engaged in our larger charter of funding significant projects."

The megacommunity also found it useful to engage what Schubert calls "the philanthropic side." According to Schubert, "That's a really good source of funding. It's a different type of funding. It tends to be longer term. And whereas business wants the return on investment in relation to business, philanthropies want the return on investment that's related to the Great Barrier Reef, to be specific. And that's, in many ways, an easier sell for us, and less resource intensive, with the very, very limited resources that we have. So that was always the plan. So we brought on a philanthropist to start to advise us on how we should approach the philanthropic sector. And, you know, our business plan has already had some success. A year or more away from now, we're going to move into the public sphere. In every aspect, our approach to the threats faced by the Reef is a phased process, regarding what we're attacking and where our priorities are."

The Reef megacommunity was not only resourceful about their funding structure; they were also extremely innovative in their development of an operational structure. In terms of pure network capability, they influenced the development of a new hub that could facilitate the coordination of many of their internal activities. According to Judith Stewart, Managing Director of the Great Barrier Reef Foundation, "There are sixteen research institutions on the Reef. One way in which they have now linked is through the MTSRF—the Marine & Tropical Research Facility, a AU $40 million fund which the Australian government has established to fund research which will protect the environmental assets of North Queensland and in particular the Reef, the rainforest and the Torres Straits."

The MTSRF was established as a direct result of the strategic planning and priority setting exercises that the Foundation initiated back in 2004. The MTSRF funds multi-institutional projects and teams working on an annual research program that addresses the major threats. "In this sense," says Stewart, "there is ongoing collaboration, ongoing consensus on how best to address the threats and some efficiencies in how funding is allocated and spent."

Meanwhile, the foundation's focus on the corporate sector, and particularly on engaging with the chief executives and chairmen of leading Australian companies, has delivered more than just fundraising results. It has enabled the foundation to educate businesses about the major threats to the Reef, raise awareness about the Reef's particular vulnerability to these threats, and bring the scientists into the realm of business, allowing them the chance to talk with one another across the table. "While this has had a direct fundraising result," says Stewart, "it has also meant that high level business leaders now know what we are doing, and what we are up against."

The success of the Great Barrier Reef Foundation demonstrates one way in which a megacommunity might begin to push beyond the identification of stakeholders toward the articulation of goals, the building of a foundation, and the implementation of action. And it certainly demonstrates, as we've said, that there are some problems for which the megacommunity approach is the only solution.

As the Great Barrier Reef example also shows, when the "overlap of vital interests" has been acknowledged, and "convergence" becomes concrete, the megacommunity itself will move on to a new set of challenges. These are best defined as challenges of structure and sustainability, and most clearly embodied in the development of rules, tools, and capabilities. In other words: Now that we've found each other, what exactly do we do?

As we discovered, every megacommunity will be different. Some megacommunities may structure themselves more strictly and formally than others. Enel, for example, has initiated a very "formal" megacommunity around the issue of energy and new infrastructures in the Vereto, complete with evaluation charts and an operating manual. On the other hand, Hewlett-Packard has initiated a more informal megacommunity around the issue of education in Africa, relying on less codified, but equally dedicated, networks and collaborations. The structure of the Great Barrier Reef megacommunity lies somewhere in the middle.

Your own structure and approach will reflect the issues involved, the people involved, and the environment in which the megacommunity must operate. However, all effective megacommunity approaches have two things in common: a pragmatic bias toward action, and time and effort set aside for reflection.

Much has been learned during the past four decades about collective learning: the building of capacities by people working together in either an organization or a community. Megacommunity design draws directly on that body of knowledge, and its core hallmark is the design of action and reflection together.[2]

As this body of knowledge makes clear, every meeting or gathering, whether informal or formal, should have two purposes:

The first purpose is to move toward the goal (action). A megacommunity has come together to solve a problem. Participants and sponsors will only have the patience to continue if you can consistently demonstrate progress. You don't have to solve the problem all at once; indeed, you can't. But you can visibly improve conditions, starting with the "low-hanging fruit" (the easiest and fastest gains), and moving on to more long-lasting and fundamental successes.

The second purpose of meetings is to educate the participants, to demonstrate continued and increasing competence and skill. This requires reflection. Your ability to solve problems will only expand as you gain awareness, mastering the ability to see what you have done and what you are doing, as others might see it. Small groups are the most effective way to build this capability, if they meet regularly to talk candidly about the way they think and work. This, by the way, is a hallmark of operations at the most effective workplace environments we know, such as that at Toyota (where management engages production line workers in frequent meetings on ways to improve efficiency and effectiveness). But Toyota's operations take place within a single organization and a single sector. In a megacommunity, the process is more diverse, more difficult, and more exhilarating.

The core group's task at hand is design; not the design of a solution, per se, but the design of the forums, practices, prototypes, and experiments through which a solution will emerge. In every one of the participating organizations, there will be many sub-teams with multiple professional backgrounds; teams working on marketing, logistics, production, training, communications, and purchasing, teams of legal, medical, engineering, educational, financial, and management professionals, and teams with formal mandates and informal teams. In the megacommunity structure, members of these teams step forward into working groups that explore solutions. They remain in the working groups for three reasons: 1) because they value the engagement they find there; 2) because they value the increased capabilities that megacommunities bring to bear on an issue; and 3) because they see that they are accomplishing something.

ARTICULATE GUIDING PRINCIPLES

From the outset, megacommunity leaders will need to articulate (and thereby test) some general principles for guiding the behavior of those within the megacommunity. For example, in some communities or on some topics, it may be necessary to say that the megacommunity is bound by the rule of law. This may be important to propose explicitly in some cultures, because the megacommunity is also a vehicle for sidestepping some of the bureaucratic and reflexively obstructionist practices that naturally occur in many communities. Therefore, the appearance of being above the law is fatal. No one is proposing that megacommunities—despite their call for close association and negotiation—flout antitrust laws, for example, or laws regarding collusion. Nothing in the idea of a megacommunity would sanction illegal behavior. Each megacommunity should propose its own set of internal rules, a set of understandings that become more refined as people engage and experiment, coalescing into guidelines for order and governance.

As George Yong-Boon Yeo, Singapore's minister of Foreign Affairs, expressed in our interview: "In order to plug in . . . you need the ethical codes. You need the rules of proper conduct and you need dispute resolution." Yet Yeo warns us that "these things will never replace the deep legacy, which is your deep internal operating system. You can never meddle too much in those because those things are products of very prolonged and complex historical evolution." Keeping this reality check in mind, we have developed some guiding principles that will be effective in megacommunities.

1) RESPECT THE AUTONOMY OF EACH PLAYER WITHIN THE NETWORK

When operating within a megacommunity, it is extremely important to remember that organizations maintain their autonomy outside the megacommunity. This is a critical concept, underscored by Foreign Minister Yeo's caveat. Member organizations should not be criticized for carrying out objectives within their own organizations that are not part of the shared vital interest.

It's already self-evident that member organizations are free to join the megacommunity at whatever point in the network they want, for whatever duration they would like, and at whatever level of resource commitment makes sense to them. But they need to recognize that each participant is bound by some unique constraints—based on their particular industry, sector, and geographic location—and those constraints will affect their approach to the problems at hand.

Private negotiations among members (including the formation of public–private partnerships, or other such partnerships) are allowed. However, once such negotiations result in an official partnership, it should be publicized to all members.

Respecting an organization's autonomy also means respecting its opinions. In any productive relationship, whether you're discussing a business contract or a marriage, it's necessary to respect the opinions of others. In the megacommunity context, disagreement will occur, but it is important to keep in mind that the ability to disagree is granted to all.

2) SHARE A COMMITMENT TO CONTACT, COMMUNICATE, AND ENGAGE

There must be a commitment to organize on behalf of the whole. As part of this commitment, there must be a commitment of time and personnel as well. When people in the megacommunity try to understand what optimizing means to them, they will be looking for evidence that others have made a commitment and understand how to keep it. Thus, there must be a commitment to openly share all information central to the vital interest at hand.

3) REMAIN BIASED TOWARD ACTION

Megacommunities don't exist to admire a problem. They are there to take action. In a megacommunity, action takes many forms. Some examples of these types of action include addressing the vital interest, keeping the megacommunity's overlapping vital interests conspicuous, and running the day-to-day operations of the megacommunity.

In some cases, actions will be defined as agreed-upon levels of group performance. In other cases, actions can be defined by your own singular plans. If this occurs, you must communicate how your actions will optimize the interests of the megacommunity as a whole and how it fits into the network and the megacommunity's progress. Consider the megacommunity-like actions that have occurred around the issue of global resources in Antarctica, for example. The organizations involved—including research institutes, government agencies, nonprofits, tourism operators, and fishing companies—do not share the same incentives for having a stake in the issue at hand, or maintain complete agreement about the methods for achieving a particular mission. The members have a wide array of perspectives about how the region's resources should be managed. Yet they have all remained committed to actions that would not override anyone else's distinct concerns.

For example, small-scale "expedition tourism" has existed since 1957 and is currently subject to the requirements of the Antarctic Treaty and Environmental Protocol, which has not come fully into force. But because of the strong overlapping vital interests in both environmental protection and safety, the expeditions are in effect self-regulated by the International Association of Antarctica Tour Operators (IAATO). The guiding principle in the protocol is that all activities should be planned and conducted on the basis of information sufficient to evaluate their possible impact on the Antarctic environment and its associated ecosystems, and on the value of Antarctica for the conduct of scientific research. In making decisions about structuring an expedition, organizers—under the scrutiny of the IAATO—strive to balance environmental impact and scientific research. In fact, the Environmental Protocol requires that "activities shall be modified, suspended or cancelled if they result in or threaten to result in impacts upon the Antarctic environment or dependent or associated ecosystems."[3] This respect for potentially competing interests allows for the sustainability of the megacommunity. To arrive at actionable decisions, each organization's megacommunity liaison—or group of liaisons—must have the proper level of authority. They should not have to always pass all their actions through a board or CEO-like figure.

There should be a commitment to avoiding intentional disruption of the system or progress toward the shared mission. Although megacommunities should include adversarial groups as part of its stakeholder system, and this dynamic tension will indeed be harnessed by the megacommunity, those adversaries should be intent on using the megacommunity context to find common ground. If that is not their intent, they are not inherently part of the megacommunity. We see the adversarial nature of megacommunities as something akin to what happens in a courtroom, where opposing counsel are adversarial but remain committed to justice being served.

COLLOQUY AND CONFLICT

Stating principles will inevitably raise questions of conflict: How do we enforce these principles within a megacommunity, and how do we deal with someone who egregiously violates them?

No one should be looking to eliminate conflict. Conflict is normal. As Jennifer Windsor, executive director of Freedom House, points out: "You're not going to change each organization completely. They're going to do certain things to annoy you and that's okay. That's what goes with the terrain."

Within a megacommunity, conflict should not to be avoided and tamped down at first indicator. The problem exists, in part, because conflicts exist. Conflicts exist between corporations and environmental groups, between management and labor unions, and between two different organizations with claims on the same profit center or resource, such as the same parcel of land. All of these organizations have reason to mistrust each other, and paradoxically, the way they begin to resolve that mistrust is not by ignoring or suppressing it, but by candidly and dispassionately talking about the reasons why it exists.

Conflicts need not lead to the vilification of a disputant. We are not looking for reasons to blame someone. Conflicts should be seen as part of the glue that holds the community together. After all, constant negotiation—a central tenet of megacommunity—means constant conflict. Parties work through the conflict in frank discussions, and in the "permanent negotiation" formats made familiar through conflict resolution and group dynamics techniques.

Opposers *can* be valuable participants, because they can provide a warning of the unintended "side effects" and implications of any forward-looking idea. That warning would otherwise not be heard. But there may be times when conflict reaches a degree of destructiveness that threatens internal convergence. That is less likely to happen in an active megacommunity, because in networks, disruptive nodes tend to be neglected, lose their links, and cease to be a member of the megacommunity. This natural delinking amounts to a de facto expulsion from the megacommunity.

In practice—and just as the field of conflict resolution would suggest—most disagreements can reach a harmonious conclusion if they are approached professionally. The value of the megacommunity process is that it tends to raise disagreements early, when it's easier to resolve them, and it provides people a context of mutual concern (practitioners of dialogue call this a "container," a term coined by physicist David Bohm) that makes resolution easier still.

THE ROLE OF "ROLES"

As we move toward structuring the megacommunity, there are many possible roles we can imagine. While we use the terms initiator, hub, and node to describe the *structural* role of megacommunity participants, we can also project the need for a broader, richer set of *functional* roles, including:

- Program managers who oversee particular projects;
- Media directors, who design, write, and manage the Web site through which the megacommunity communicates with others;
- Media liaisons, who maintain connection with journalists, editors, broadcasters, and other media professionals;
- Subject matter experts, responsible for keeping the other participants informed about technical, scientific, or other specialized

areas of interest. This may take the form of an advisory board, a team of experts that gather to discuss subject matter with an independent eye and supply what everyone can agree are objective recommendations.

Specific functional roles will vary with each specific megacommunity. But there is only one type of functional role that is imperative. Each participating entity has to have a primary representative—or set of representatives—interfacing with the megacommunity, a point person for external engagement contacts. Microsoft, for example, has done this with many of its local initiatives around the world. It has redesigned their business so that their in-country managers are able to address a wide variety of issues, pursue overlaps in vital interests, and be points of contact to particular organizations, thus linking those groups directly back to the company's head, ensuring communication up and down the line.

This point person has both "outside-in" and "inside-out" functions. Within the megacommunity, these representatives will act as liaisons—ready contacts—between the megacommunity and the organizations that make up the megacommunity. One of the ways Enel, for example, built on the lessons learned in Brindisi, was to create just this kind of liaison position in the Veneto. This liaison—which they chose to call a "megacommunity manager"—was appointed with the sweeping task of supporting engineering and institutional relations as well as communication processes, overseeing the clarity of messaging, positioning, and data provided to the megacommunity. At the same time, a chosen liaison should ensure the application of megacommunity processes and management *within* his or her organization, as well as enabling megacommunity-related information to flow inside their organizations.

As for other functional roles, liaisons are responsible for doing what it is they do best. Entities will act from the basis of capabilities. In fact, in a megacommunity, functional roles are synonymous with capabilities and activities, as they align with the specific, time-sensitive need of the megacommunity to address the overlap of vital interests. Taking a "snapshot" of a megacommunity will reveal that some organizations have provided "thought leaders" (that is, those who offer new insight and concepts) while others have provided ground-level operators or key negotiators among nodes, for example. But this static picture does not capture the dynamism of the "real" megacommunity where there is a constant shifting of resources to meet the needs of any given moment. In a megacommunity, roles are not tattooed on your arms. (Over time, the megacommunity may need different *initiators* for different *initiatives* on-going within the megacommunity.) Roles—such as they are— will be very varied and dynamic. Any specific role will evolve, as do all roles in the megacommunity, but it will remain directly related to an individual's current and political capabilities.

In no way should involvement in the megacommunity be perceived as pro bono work, since megacommunity actions directly affect the success of each member organization. In fact, given the importance of any megacommunity's central issue, it is likely that a participating organization has already committed time and resources to solving that issue. Megacommunity involvement may simply represent a reorienting of this effort, to better effect.

THE ART AND SCIENCE OF CROSS-SECTOR ENGAGEMENT

Having established the need for rules and roles, we can now get to the heart of any megacommunity: the active promotion of cross-sector engagement. A design, over time, of increasing mutual engagement is the essence of megacommunity. Among other things, it allows for complimentary capabilities to be revealed and mobilized. This dynamism will surely lead to a more sustainable level of problem-solving, as well as a new level of capacity-building on the part of everyone involved (capacity-building being one of the key benefits of joining a megacommunity).

In every community, there is something to be traded. A megacommunity trades on such capital as strategic intellect, areas of expertise, efficacy of operations, connections, and leadership. But the true scope and potential of this capital will be more vividly revealed if the megacommunity develops exercises, structures, and tools for fostering and sustaining collective action, some of which we have detailed below.

These can be formal relationship-building exercises that define roles, actions, partner clusters, etc., delivered by a professional; or the exercises can be as simple as round-table conversations, conducted around a vital question such as: "What is our working hypothesis about the fundamental nature of the problem?" Relationship-building exercises can go a long way toward giving the megacommunity's vital interest more clarity and more nuance at the same time. Some theories and mechanisms have proven more successful than others, and each megacommunity will have a natural affinity for one or another, particularly if some leaders have experience with a particular approach. In our work, we've found four approaches to be highly effective.

1) Develop a Meeting Schedule. Frequent contact is key to the operation of the megacommunity. So while it may seem obvious that meetings must take place, they are unlikely to occur of their own accord. For this reason, it's imperative to be proactive, and very structured, in that regard. Thus, as a first step, a megacommunity must define a workable schedule of meetings over time—and all members must strive, as best they can, for full attendance. In many ways, adherence to this schedule will be the first demonstration of commitment.

2) Employ Strategic Simulations. Games and strategic simulations can be spectacularly effective in uncovering complementing capabilities. In these simulations, stakeholders join together to play out fabricated crises occurring around their area of vital interest. These kinds of games, which are generally designed by professionals to simulate the way in which a crisis might realistically unfold, allow groups to play out the ramifications of their decisions. Some decisions, after all, will (according to the game) make the crisis less damaging; others will make it worse. The games foster cascading dialogues in which small groups can grapple with pieces of the puzzle, and discover the areas in which they can be most effective. A strategic simulation will uncover strengths and weaknesses, and it will go a long way toward defining key actions that can be taken outside the simulation.

In short, a strategic simulation can take a mind-numbingly complex issue (a global dynamics issue, let's say, that is only understood at a high theoretical level) and render it approachable for action. "Gaming out" a scenario is a relatively risk-free process that challenges conventional wisdom and allows participants to break with "known truths" and past assumptions.

In chapter two, we described a strategic simulation that Booz Allen co-led around the issue of HIV/AIDS in India. In another simulation, conducted in December 2001, representatives from all three sectors explored innovative ideas and practical solutions to bioterrorism in a strategic simulation conducted in Washington, D.C. The event was designed to proactively improve the awareness of participants and increase our nation's capabilities in preparedness and response to bioterrorism. The overlapping vital interest was clear, as was the challenge: Was the United States prepared to cope with a bioterrorist attack? Specifically, what if terrorists released an aerosolized pneumonic plague bacteria—a deadly virus in a spray can—simultaneously in two major cities in a coordinated attack?

Just as megacommunity initiators identify and enlist a salient set of cross-sector stakeholders, the wargame brought together senior policymakers in the Department of Health and Human Services, the Federal Emergency Management Agency, the Department of Defense, the Department of Veterans Affairs, and state and local government. The wargame enlisted participants from the business community including CEOs and senior executives in medical products companies, including pharmaceuticals and biotechnology. Healthcare providers, insurers, and the Red Cross also took part.

The players were organized into teams representing key business and government sectors, with a mix of government and business people

assigned to each team. The mixed groups gave individuals a rapid education in how other organizations think and act, as well as providing a
first check on ideas and suggestions.

Teams faced several dilemmas in responding to the simulated
bioterrorism event. Clearly, the extreme contagiousness of plague and
the lack of a vaccine, called for both quarantine (or "protective isolation") and the rapid and extensive prophylactic treatment of uninfected
individuals with antibiotics. But quarantining thousands of people at
once raised civil liberties and law enforcement issues, while widespread
prophylaxis strained drug supplies and left the country vulnerable to
new attacks or naturally occurring epidemics.

Working together, participants had to deal with choices, dilemmas,
and the consequences of their actions, as well as identify next steps to
improve real-world coordination and capabilities in response to a bioterrorism scenario. One of their most important conclusions involved the
widespread recognition of the need for a new kind of partnership in the
pursuit of homeland security. Preparedness would require new levels of
communication and cooperation across public–private, local–national,
and military–civilian boundaries. In other words, their findings showed
that they, themselves, were a latent megacommunity—and one that
would need deliberate design to move into action.

3) Develop Targeted Forums. Large, cross-sector meetings and conferences can also be an effective means of relationship-building in the early
stages. These forums should not be confused with regular meetings of
the megacommunity. They should be much more time-intensive, spe-

cific events that ask participants to come together for several days. And they should be organized to reflect what is best and most productive about the forum model.

In our discussion with Victor Fung, the group chairman of the Li & Fung group of companies, he criticized forums that have no "clear message," where there's "no focus." That is a complaint commonly heard in our interviews. Megacommunity forums need to be built around specific agendas. Every meeting should have an articulated theme. And yet megacommunities should also avoid conducting forums with the standard "packed-in" conference format of presentations and panel discussions. The primary purpose of these forums should be to build relationships and help participants develop the ability to work together. That ability will atrophy if people only hear each other's formal speeches.

In his long experience, Ian Buchanan, senior executive advisor to Booz Allen Hamilton, has found forums to be very useful in untangling "cause and effect, symptoms from fact." And while he points out that "you need forums," he also feels that "you need somebody who is skilled at it. You can call it leadership. You can call it facilitation, whatever you wish. But it is a distinct skill set." Thus, Buchanan anticipates another potential functional role for someone in the megacommunity.

The actual structure of these forums will depend on the needs of the specific megacommunity. But every meeting should include a statement (or re-statement) of the overlapping vital interest. We would also suggest that the structure of these meetings allow for what Fulvio Conti, CEO of Enel, refers to as "open dialogue." ("These dialogues," according to Conti, "could become highly opinionated and confrontational but they have to happen so that you can create leaders and a common development path.") We would also suggest that while the goal of the earliest megacommunity meetings may be to foster relationships, these meetings should move quickly toward stressing the development of organized initiatives, action strategies, and their implementation.

There are several structures for open dialogue that megacommunities have found useful. Most common is the "Future Search" model written about by pioneers in the field of organizational development, such as Marvin Weisbord, Barbara Bunker, Billie Alban, and many others. This model has its roots in socio-technical systems and organizational development. Typically lasting two or three days, these conferences alternatively converge in large plenary sessions and break out into smaller working groups, considering some variation of three main questions: What do we aspire to? What is our current reality? And how can we get from here to there?

Another common model, which has been used with surprisingly powerful results, is the "Open Space" meeting developed by author and organizational consultant Harrison Owen. The invited participants show up without an agenda. Each individual has the option of proposing a topic, and people gravitate to the topics they think are important. If they are bored or reach a conclusion, they drift on (or move on) to other parts of the gathering. "Whoever comes are the right people," Owen has written. "Whatever happens is the only thing that could have. Whenever it starts is the right time. When it's over, it's over."

A third model, developed by authors Juanita Brown and David Isaacs, has been dubbed the "World Café." Different tables or groups act as hosts, with some people staying in one topic area and others moving from place to place at designated hours, with the purpose adjusting as time passes.

All of these models are improved with expert facilitation. And over the years, facilitators have learned ways to inspire commonality and the kind of depth needed to understand problems. Some simple techniques can make a big difference. For example, "checking in" gives every participant a chance to say something, by going from person to person around in a circle, right at the beginning. This has the effect of legitimizing everyone present, and setting the conversation on a flowing and productive course. A check-in is never a waste of time.

Another technique involves setting a simple ground rule that, rather than interrupting others or "waiting for my turn to speak," each speaker will pause to count a beat before leaping into the conversation. This adds a deliberative and respectful tone to the conversation, and it also raises the bar of the conversation. Comments tend to be much more considered and coherent, even after only half a beat. And they are generally more creative as well.

These types of ground rules, and others like them, help ensure that megacommunity forums are action-oriented, resulting in the establishment of hard goals to be met. And they also help participants to be more reflective in general, providing—as Eric Levine, CEO of Students Partnership Worldwide, calls it—"a flexible concept of looking at their own house."

"I think the problem with forums," Levine says, "is that everyone coming to the table has to be willing to evaluate their own practices and behaviors. And I think that that's very rare."

4) Prototype teams. A megacommunity may involve dozens, even hundreds of people working toward a mutual goal. It may be easier to divide them into cross-sector, cross-organization teams where they can identify and focus on nested projects or subtasks. Regard each of these subtasks as an experiment, or if you prefer, a prototype. Whether it succeeds or fails, you will learn from it, reflect on it, and apply its lesson to the next round of activities. Every participating organization should have at least two or three people involved, sometimes many more, each in a different prototyping team. The assignments need to be loose enough to permit creativity, but tight enough to fit into the overall goals.

THE CREATIVE DEPLOYMENT OF INFORMATION TECHNOLOGY

In the 1970s, the phrase "appropriate technology" was used in nonprofit circles to describe tools and machines—such as passive solar buildings—that did not require massive industrialization. But it is no longer possible to distinguish between "big technology" and "small technology" in the same way. The major reason for this is the advent of the personal computer and the Internet, which have irreversibly blurred the boundaries between "big" and "small" machines. And they are helping to bridge the gaps among the public, private, and civil sectors as well.

Since Internet technology contributes to so many of the issues of complexity that make megacommunity necessary, it's appropriate, perhaps, that the Internet might provide one of our best tools for solving some of these problems. Depending on the specific tools employed, the Internet and various information technology (IT) tools can be used to foster the idea of permeable boundaries, allow fluid information flow (that is, reporting), and generally enable continual engagement. Certainly, no one would deny that the Internet is a new media that must be mastered in a globalized world. Integrating the creative use of this new medium is a central feature of effective megacommunity designs.

Many people involved in a megacommunity are already deeply involved in the new worlds of multiparticipant media—which includes wikis, blogs, massive multiplayer online games, self-publishing media, virtual worlds, and more. Cyberspace, after all, has become the new version of a classic "commons"—the new coffee house.

Communication channels such as texting, instant messaging, mobile photo blogging, and location-aware services will add a new sense of dynamism to a megacommunity. In fact, one reason the megacommunity concept is viable in the first place is the ability of telecommunications to supply ongoing contact without a huge outlay of time, and without constantly hopping on planes and trains.

There is no reason why a megacommunity could not use the MySpace, Friendster, or Facebook environment or invent its own version. A megacommunity could choose to have a wide-open system (like MySpace) or a more tented system (like Facebook where you can control who sees each piece of information you provide). This system could be used to post all sorts of information relevant to the megacommunity's efficient and effective functioning. In the early phases of a megacommunity's life, and as part of relationship building, members might use their cyber-social environment to distribute something of a "wish list" to other members, regarding their reasons for joining the megacommunity. This list would publicize expectations and galvanize results, while helping to telescope future actions on the part of all participants.

As the megacommunity develops, it can use its cyber-environment to post and retrieve all types of information—including simple contact information, dashboard tools, regularly updated progress reports, and strategic plans. Reporting, in fact, is a key element of monitoring in the megacommunity. It goes toward the megacommunity's continued commitment to transparency, and also its need for pooling capacities and information. It can keep the entire megacommunity abreast of collaborative initiatives, providing everyone with the data culled by those in the megacommunity who take "the deep dive into issues"—as Michael MacIntyre, from the Harvard Initiative for Global Health, calls it.

Cyber-reporting can also keep everyone informed on what's working and what isn't on a real-time basis, as those dynamics play out. And, as Barbara Waugh of HP suggests, the megacommunity's efforts could and should be cross-referenced for both "local and broad-scale integration and impact."

Depending on the formality of your approach to megacommunity maintenance, you may also consider exploring issue-tracking software, the creation of shared databases, shared workspaces, and media plans. The megacommunity may even find a way to use its cyber-environment to resolve conflict. The possibilities are seemingly endless, restricted only by your imagination and knowledge of what's out there.

THE NEED FOR A COMMON LANGUAGE

As relationships build in a megacommunity, there should also be a conscious movement toward defining some kind of common language. People from each of the three sectors tend to have different ways of phrasing the same statement; indeed, preferred language varies even from corporation to corporation, or from function to function. The differences can be profound. They go beyond just the linguistic treatment of communications, to the underlying ways of thinking that shape those communications.

Imagine, for example, the head of a public works department who sits down with his director of IT services to talk about a new software tool that processes, say, customer requests. The public works person might express concerns about issues such as "mean-time-to-failure for key pieces of mechanical equipment" while the baffled IT person might respond in terms of "graphical user interfaces." (Add the fact that, most likely, they would be using mind-addling acronyms such as "MTF" and "GUI.") This is a simple example, but it shows just how divergent language can be, even within the same organization.

Here is an expanded version of a table originally developed by Waugh at Hewlett-Packard, generally spelling out the different ways that people from each of the three sectors talk and think. (See figure 5.1 on page 172.)

As you set a megacommunity course—and navigate the waters—there has to be some way to understand the language and thus the expectations of the other members. Among other things, a shared agreement about terms and language ("let us agree that when we say,

FIGURE 5.1

FEATURE	BUSINESSES	CIVIL SOCIETY	GOVERNMENT
Paradigm for change	Organization development	Community organizing	Mandate from constituents
Structure	Hierarchy	Informal network	Formal network
Sources of leadership	Position in the hierarchy (a senior VP outranks a director)	Influence over the network (a gardener can be the leader if knowledge of gardening is critical)	Political proximity (a minister or cabinet secretary's "inner circle" calls the shots)
Leadership method	Bold directives	Big Questions	Big Programs
Sources of connection among people	Reporting relationship	Trust	Mission area
Source of disconnect	Reorganization	Betrayal	Marginalizing
Style of communication	Broadcasting messages; getting "buy-in" and then executing top-down strategies	Listening at all levels, in-depth conversations, creating strategy together before proceeding	Studying an issue, examining options, formal policy / position development and dissemination
Approach to strategy	Setting objectives and then "driving to the end point"	Discovery through successive approximation; "we learn where we're going as we travel"	Determine objectives from indicators, distribute execution responsibility
Management method	Project management	Probability-driven experimentation	People management
Approach to planning	Precise, linear, step by step processes	Cycles of action and reflection, deliberately disruptive moves	Formalistic, stylized and tradition-linked processes
Approach to change	Plan it, manage it	Catalyze the emergence of something new	Change only on a grand scale
How decisions are made	Leader decides	Consensus emerges	Decisions emerge from groups

'consensus,' we are talking about any decision where there is enough agreement to move forward") can be useful in sharing and aligning business models, which will help immensely in the operational sense. And it's needed to make sure that despite the many different perspectives folding into a megacommunity, there is some common way of looking at the megacommunity as a whole. A common language is also necessary for measuring the progress of the megacommunity, that is, developing a set of common metrics. (See the discussion of metrics later in this chapter.)

Participants gradually bridge such boundaries by learning, as dialogue expert William Isaacs suggests, to "suspend" their assumptions—not to mask them, but to voice them dispassionately and allow them to be visible to all, as if suspended on a platform in the middle of the room. A common language will certainly begin to emerge through the process of relationship-building, through time spent talking together. Over time, continued interactions will lead—in a passive manner, almost through osmosis—to better understanding. It will certainly lead to enhanced linguistic abilities and fresh intellectual pathways.

In this regard, there are certain conversational objectives to keep in mind:

- Try to gain a clear understanding of the other party's perspective and objectives. If the objectives and motivation of the other party are not clear to you, ask for clarification.
- Focus on areas on which you both agree.
- Focus on the resolutions each party sees as fair.

- Be explicit about your determination to find a mutually satisfactory resolution.
- Voice your appreciation of the work the other party has put into fixing the problem.

But there are more dynamic, less passive methods for arriving at a common language. A rigorous megacommunity might consider the deployment of a few useful analytic tools such as those used in "value chain analysis" and "visualization."

VALUE CHAIN ANALYSIS

In the business world, value chain analysis has proven to provide a common language for members of a diverse community with different backgrounds and perspectives. First discussed as such by Harvard University Professor Michael Porter in his 1985 bestseller *Competitive Advantage: Creating and Sustaining Superior Performance,* the value chain framework has become a powerful and popular analytic tool for strategic planning.[4]

Used by a single organization, a value chain is the network of operations that makes it possible for organizations to produce the service for which they are chartered. Basically, "value chain analysis" refers to the categorization and depiction of these generic activities linked together, so that an organization better understands how, where, and when activity occurs within an organization. It provides a "bird's eye view" of the processes and action steps an organization undertakes to meet its objectives. By representing the processes and action steps as discreet and understandable activities, one does not need expert knowledge to understand their role and importance in the overall scheme.

Consider this example of a value chain, one found in many consumer-oriented manufacturing businesses. (See figure 5.2.)

In each of these activities, value can be added, lost, improved upon, exposed to risk, etc. By changing the amount and quality of information flowing along the value chain, firms may try to bypass the intermediaries, create new business models or, in other ways, improve its value system. For example, a manufacturer might come to understand that its parts suppliers should be located nearby its assembly plant to minimize the cost of transportation.

FIGURE 5.2: VALUE CHAIN

Product Design	Procurement	Factory Planning & Production	Distribution	Sales & Marketing	Customer Service
•Market feedback	•Strategic sourcing	•Capacity planning	•Finished goods delivery	•Marketing calls	•Customer care
•Design for manufactur- ability/opera- tions	•Inventory management	•Demand forecast	•Shipping costs	•Cross-selling opportunities	•Support costs
	•Distributed procurement	•Utilization and throughput	•Warehousing	•Channel management	•Account management
		•Distributed manufacturing	•Transport optimization	•Promotions	

The figure illustrates the value chain for a typical manufacturing business. The value chain contains the set of operations that makes it possible for the businesses to manufacture the product that they are in business to produce.

Source: Booz Allen Hamilton

The value chain framework quickly made its way to the forefront of management thought by providing a way for diverse elements of a company to communicate with each other about what they do or plan on doing. Each department now had a way to understand the implications of its actions in a company-wide manner.

In a megacommunity, the value chain concept can be extended to incorporate all three sectors. Consider, for example, the value chain associated with the area of food safety in the United States. Food security uses a systematic approach to protect the food network that involves all three sectors. As shown in figure 5.3, there is a shared responsibility across the sectors for protecting the delivery network from damage to its product (the food), from damage to its processes (the ability to continue to supply food), and from being turned into a weapon system for mass casualties and economic destruction. This already makes for a very complex value system. The systems only grows more complex when you consider the need to conduct inspection, surveillance, and diagnosis, the need to respond to public health and economic viability issues, and the need to oversee investigations and enforce legal authority.

Porter describes this larger interconnected system of value chains as the "value system," and it's in this incarnation that the concept finds its megacommunity application. A value system includes the value chains of a firm's supplier (and their suppliers all the way back), the firm itself, the firm distribution channels, and the firm's buyers (and presumably extends to the buyers of their products, and beyond). From a company perspective, this means enabling the other constituencies to identify their claims along a value chain that produces benefits for all. In this way, it can help a megacommunity build a common language.

FIGURE 5.3: THE FOOD SECURITY
VALUE CHAIN AT THE STATE LEVEL

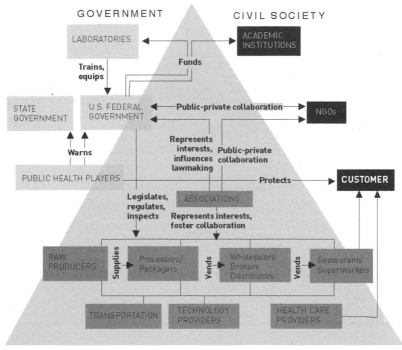

This rendering of the value chain for food security demonstrates the range of stakeholders in the issue, as well as the complex set of relationships among stakeholders. This is a partial list for demonstration purposes only.

Source: Booz Allen Hamilton

Value system analysis produces an activity map of the megacommunity. This gives people a better context for communicating. ("Okay, what do you mean by 'production' in this step of your value chain?") ("To me, product innovation and R&D are the same step.") This new context will help the megacommunity take significant steps toward further convergence and toward structure. It also ensures that the megacommunity reflects and honors the short- and long-term goals of all its participants by using those goals to build the activity map of the megacommunity. And it might impart the first truly comprehensive (and thus validating) statement of a megacommunity's aspirations.

VISUALIZING THE NETWORK

While all healthy megacommunities should have a similarly robust dynamic, they will not necessarily have the same shape. That's where another analytic tool comes into play: visualization.

Throughout the life of a megacommunity, visualization is a way of seeing the megacommunity in its entirety. In the initiation phase, visualization has an element of projection. It shows the connections that could exist if the latent megacommunity became active. These tools can be used to imagine the appropriate scale and shape for a megacommunity and model it, in a simple network sense. Megacommunity members must ask themselves what shape their network might take. Will there be lots of hubs and nodes? One hub and many nodes? Does it make sense to create a hub where none exists (as done by the Great Barrier Reef megacommunity)? Do they want a network with only one hub and 700 nodes? Or do they want hubs to share risk with other hubs?

These simple visual projections of a megacommunity's possible future shape can aid in determining its first actions. They can help you decide, for example, who to introduce to each other. If the lines of connection are sparse between two member organizations, a megacommunity might probably want to introduce more meetings among those two groups.

Then, once the megacommunity is up and running, visualization tools can be used to a much more dynamic effect, and provide a wider range of important information. They move out into a more complex type of modeling that shows relationships in more detail, and can be most useful in determining a sense of the megacommunity's engagement patterns.

They can define certain "network neighborhoods," define short and long paths of influence and connection, identify strong ties and weak ties, offer cluster analysis, and provide a sense of influence and prestige. They offer an excellent way of assessing active participants, and of identifying latent elements as well.

A good network mapping tool can provide an accurate picture of how a specific hub is functioning in a megacommunity, recalling that a hub not only has myriad connections, but by its very nature is connected on different levels (as a supplier, customer, regulatee, etc.) with many other bodies. Given their potential for influence, it is worth identifying hubs and involving them early in megacommunity activities.

In other words, visualization can help a megacommunity decide who to reach out to and in what order. It allows a megacommunity's constituents to see who they are connected to, who they need to be connected to, and who they want to be connected to. It will also show them who is connected to who—and how. If they want direct access to a hub (as we've seen small nonprofits seek around many issues, such as water scarcity), they may chose to link directly to a large company. If they are interested in using linkages with other nodes to get access to information, they may simply link to another node (as we've seen around the issue of avian flu, where a small company links into a local initiative that passes on information about avian flu emergency preparedness).

But visualization will not only help a megacommunity make decisions about its actions within the megacommunity. It will also help the megacommunity make informed decisions within its own organization. For example, if a megacommunity can clearly visualize its closest links, it can project that, for the most part, their links' constraints are theirs as well. (Going back to the idea of each organization posting a "wish list," a good visualization tool should point out whose "wish list" a megacommunity really needs to read.)

Visualization tools will also allow the megacommunity to determine the strength or fragility of its network. For example, the megacommunity's network may be fragile if its visualization model shows that the megacommunity is too dependent on a single hub. (A megacommunity should be able to survive the loss of any one member.) On the other hand, a large number of links with a wide variety of paths to various parts of the network makes it robust. Connection on multilevels is an intrinsic part of healthy network character.

Used in conjunction with "value network analysis," visualization can provide all members with a common way of looking at the megacommunity, its shape and pattern of interactions. And it moves the megacommunity toward a framework for measuring its progress.

DEFINING, MONITORING, AND MEASURING PROGRESS

A healthy megacommunity should continue to grow, developing more connections, an ever more common language, and sharply targeted action plans. But how do we define and monitor this progress over time?

In some contexts, a lowering of standards often plagues cross-sector collaboration. Participants bring less rigor to the process (including defining objectives, monitoring results, and managing the work) than they would to a project within their own organization. But in an effective megacommunity endeavor, there should be an explicit up-front level of understanding regarding what participants hope to accomplish (defining progress), what they expect to see (monitoring progress), and how they will judge success (measuring progress). In a megacommunity, all three of these concepts are inextricably bound with each other and with reflective changes in the next round of action.

ESTABLISHING MILESTONES

Progress, of course, means progress toward meeting goals. In the most general overarching sense, defining goals is relatively easy once the megacommunity's overlapping vital interest has been agreed upon—although this is not always the simplest proposition in itself. Still, once identified, the overlapping vital interest is not only the impetus for forming a megacommunity; it is also the built-in definition of success as defined by a megacommunity (examples include slowing the spread of HIV/AIDS in Uganda, finding economically viable sources of renewable energy, promoting fair trade in the coffee supply chain, etc.).

Given the complex issues around which many megacommunities form, ultimate success could be generations away. In the meantime, the megacommunity will have to define, monitor, and measure incremental successes against its overlapping vital interests. In this regard, it will help to develop a plan of action that includes milestones.

These incremental successes should appear in the form of advances that will increase the megacommunity's chances of achieving its overall goal. The megacommunity needs to ask itself: If we do the right thing, what kinds of indicators might we expect to see? Will we see improvements in revenues? Will we see an upsurge in levels of community engagement? For example, while the ultimate goal of fighting the HIV/AIDS epidemic in Uganda can naturally be judged by a lowered number of new Ugandan patients with positive HIV tests, incremental success might be judged by renewed focus from the international community, or increased awareness among Ugandans concerning the nature of the epidemic. In many cases, the more specific the overlapping vital interest, the easier it is to envision and define milestones of success.

THE NEED FOR (AND TROUBLE WITH) METRICS

Keep in mind that a megacommunity cannot assess absolute progress within itself with any finer scale than that with which it started. If the megacommunity is acting on a gut feeling that X is the problem, it won't really be able to measure progress using anything more than that gut feeling—although Ed Koch-like "How am I doin'?" measures are not without their value.[5] Still, more exacting measures and metrics can be useful, especially if the megacommunity tends toward the formal.

The trouble with metrics routes back to the differences in assumptions among public-, private-, and civil-sector professionals. Each sector, by its very nature, will measure different things—and they will have differing standards. For example, businesses engaged in the de-mining operations might measure profitability and shareholder value. An NGO might be measuring the overall number of mines removed worldwide. Meanwhile, a government may be content to simply measure the level of clean-up in their specific country.

To overcome these differences, metrics must offer transparency and relevance to the members. Each member has a "business model" and its engagement in the megacommunity cannot mean a wholesale change to its model. That would make the bar for membership too high. Therefore, megacommunity metrics have to be the combination (or integration) of those used by the members. Megacommunities must adjust their measures and metrics—through negotiation—to reflect the perspective of their connected partners while preserving the value measure from the megacommunity's perspective as a whole.

These metrics should also reflect the fact that the megacommunity is not solving the whole of the issue but rather the subset that is the overlapping vital interest for the given set of stakeholders. The megacommunity is an action-oriented activity designed to address the overlapping vital interest—to get us from point A to point B with a set of players who have a clear stake in the issue, and who have defined the problem in a way that, together, they can address it and individually benefit from addressing it. Megacommunity metrics should be defined as agreed-upon levels of performance in an agreed-upon window of performance. Mostly, these will be floor measures not ceiling ones (that is, minimum standards not maximum).

FEEDBACK MECHANISMS

Metrics must be plugged into some kind of feedback mechanism, and good feedback mechanisms are crucial to the continued health of a megacommunity. Leaders need to consciously set up feedback mechanisms that are as broad and relevant as possible. The Internet can be a major aid in following the megacommunity's progress toward hitting its milestone goals by making them easily accessible. Additionally, by monitoring all the publicly available information on the Internet, the megacommunity will be able to keep close tabs on how opinion (regarding the overlapping vital interest) is changing or evolving over time.

Feedback mechanisms also provide an opportunity for the participants to reflect together on the results, to ask themselves how they might have done better, and explore new complementary ways through which they can build on one another's skill bases. They will provide for an organizational and process check-up, so to speak. In turn, that will lead to adjustments. And adjustments will lead to sustainability. Ultimately, the bywords of megacommunity are: communicate, negotiate, act, and learn (then begin the learning cycle again).

KEEPING THE GATES OF MEMBERSHIP OPEN

A megacommunity must not only monitor its external progress against its vital interest. It must also monitor its internal health, the degree to which it is functioning effectively. The best indicator of megacommunity health may be the same as it is when measuring physical health: growth.

A megacommunity is not a gated community. A healthy megacommunity, like any healthy network, should constantly be adding new nodes and linkages. It is important to ensure that the megacommunity does not become a closed system, where the initiators determine who is in and who is not. The megacommunity must maintain the attitude that joining is essential for anyone whose work is relevant, and the barriers to entry should be, if not low, then accessible. A potential new member should not have to prove they belong in a specific megacommunity. Benefit of the doubt goes to the joiner. The burden lays with the existing network to show a strong case against a potential member—that is, a case for nonconvergence. And that case would have to be compelling to block membership.

If the megacommunity is successful, it might find itself bombarded by potential new members. And that's a good thing. It shows that the megacommunity is increasingly recognized as the central front in working toward a given vital interest. In this regard, megacommunities may find themselves acting as a force for change in profound and unexpected ways. It's not farfetched to imagine that a previously undemocratic nation's desire to be part of a particular megacommunity might begin to affect some of the country's behaviors.

New membership can only benefit the megacommunity, helping it to reach its fullest potential. Metcalfe's Law states that the value of a network is proportional to the square of the number of users of the system. In megacommunity terms, this means that as a megacommunity's nodes increase, its value increases exponentially. As the collective capacity of the megacommunity builds, it should be able to deal with ever-more complex initiatives, ensuring the sustainability of the mega-community that ensures the sustainability of globalization which, in turn, ensures sustainability of the globe.

In this regard, scaling up will often involve the taking-on of larger goals, often larger *social* goals. Or to put it plainly, most overlapping vital interests have a built-in tendency to move on several levels at the same time. As Waugh has written: "Megacommunity processes provide a natural platform for helping a region deal effectively with the goals of global competitiveness (on one hand) and the need for local quality of life and equity (on the other). As the megacommunity's work engenders foresight and awareness among the leaders of a region's organizations, they become better equipped to reconcile these seemingly incompatible objectives."

Consider the agenda set forth by the Enel/Veneto megacommu-nity. Its overlapping vital interest—sustainable energy—clearly has a scaled characteristic. In fact, it has three distinct scaling dimensions: local, national/regional, and international. The Enel/Veneto mega-community is taking the lead in understanding how local communi-ties deal with infrastructural investments and with compromise regarding, specifically, a new green coal-fuelled power generation fa-cility. It is easy to imagine that the lessons learned in the Veneto could be applied to many areas and ultimately to the larger issue of energy alternatives across the planet. Indeed, this particular megacommu-nity is beginning to show signs of actually moving in this direction. (See our Afterword.)

Scaling up can also result in an evolution of an overlapping vital interest. Lessons learned have caused Enel SpA itself to move in previously unpredictable directions. Harvard University was in the midst of exploring and strategizing how it should position its weight, charisma, and thought leadership in the context of the issue of climate change. Enel's concern with sustainable energy—as exemplified by its initiation of a megacommunity in the Veneto—led the company to endow a chair at Harvard, The Enel Endowment for Environmental Economics. The megacommunity initiated by Enel was not created to address climate change per se. But the Enel/Veneto megacommunity clearly led the utility company toward integration of this issue. Keeping one's eye on the longer term goal in this manner is critical to sustaining a megacommunity.

Scaling up and open membership also guard against certain dangers to the megacommunity. There is a theoretical potential for organizations to use megacommunity initiatives to restrict competition, thereby creating effective oligopolies (An oligopoly is a situation in which a market or industry is dominated by a small number of players.). While megacommunities form to address pressing social, economic, environmental, or health issues, one might fear that they may be exploited to provide a "goodwill" banner to protect businesses from the types of scrutiny that would normally take place when engaged in unfair competitive practices. But as structures, megacommunities guard against the negative implications of oligopolics, and it's up to the megacommunity members to make sure this remains true. The megacommunity's dedicatedly free-scale, open membership guards against the collusion of the few. There is a greater chance for effective checks and balance to emerge from a wider array of players in other sectors. And the megacommunity construct also creates opportunities for "weak links" in the network to cause direct impact, another outgrowth of scaling up. As Mark Granovetter points out, weak ties are important because they are critical to the diffusion of information and influence.

We should also point out that *as a philosophy,* a megacommunity also guards against oligopolies. After all, the market impact of collusion is the clearest form of maximizing one could imagine since the benefits of collusion come at a cost of efficiency to society. At its heart, the megacommunity drives participants toward optimizing instead of maximizing. Thus, the more that the structure of a megacommunity—from its rules to its tools—is developed with optimization in mind, in the spirit of cooperation, and with an awareness that things need to get done in a way that benefits each member and global society as a whole, the more effective that megacommunity will be.

CHAPTER 6

LEADING IN A MEGACOMMUNITY

As the need for megacommunity takes us into an ever more interdependent realm, the nature of leadership must evolve to match this new endeavor. If there is no single overarching CEO of the entire mega-program, then who exactly are we referring to when we say "megacommunity leader"? In this final chapter, we will talk about the two types of megacommunity leaders and the ten key elements of top-flight megacommunity leadership.

The first category of megacommunity leaders includes those senior leaders of organizations (e.g., CEOs, directors, chairmen, ministers) who become engaged in a megacommunity. Their full-hearted participation is crucial, because it ensures that their organizations will be fully participative. A senior leader's direct involvement will raise the commitment level of any specific node, ensuring that megacommunity attitudes and mechanisms become quickly and deeply embedded in their organization. Most people in organizations know that if a senior leader isn't visibly committed to an endeavor, it is not really a priority. And if the senior leader does not tangibly endorse a solution, it will not fly, if only because people will feel vulnerable in applying their own time and attention to it.

In tapping into a senior leader's enthusiasm, one warning applies: If a megacommunity only has the participation of one senior leader from an organization, the megacommunity will probably find itself in a somewhat vulnerable position, much like what happens in a network if it's too single-hub dependent.

To be sure, each member organization must offer someone who has the authority to commit resources. But senior leaders aren't the only ones with that ability—which brings us to our second category. This second type of leader includes the person or persons playing the role of formal liaison to the megacommunity. This liaison—which Enel, for one, has dubbed the "megacommunity manager"—has the authority to interact with the megacommunity, as well as the responsibility to carry the plans and lessons of megacommunity back to its base organization. This second category may also include people who are *informal* liaisons, who, by virtue of their role or their predisposition, are recognized for their value in connecting the individual organization to the megacommunity. For example, in environmentally oriented initiatives, heads of packaging, procurement, and facilities management find themselves cast with the opportunity to play a larger role while fulfilling their job. Some of them seize this opportunity as a way to make a contribution, establish competitive advantage for their job and their organization, and distinguish themselves. Jody Williams, campaign ambassador for the International Campaign to Ban Landmines and 1997 Nobel Peace Prize Laureate, finds, for example, that "core leaders emerged by virtue of their work." This type of engagement, in fact, is one of the things that gives megacommunities their strength.

Although there are shades of difference regarding what the megacommunity needs from senior leaders as opposed to liaisons, we've come up with ten considerations that apply to both to a large degree. Here is our list of what we see as the fundamental elements of a top-flight megacommunity leader, in the best of all possible worlds:

A SPIRIT OF INCLUSIVENESS

A megacommunity is a living embodiment of an "us *and* them" strategy, not an "us versus them" strategy. Organizations join a megacommunity to reach new levels of peak performance in finding sustainable solutions to complex issues. They recognize that these solutions will require bringing multiple frames of reference and multiple capabilities to bear. Therefore, a bias toward inclusiveness is essential on the part of a megacommunity leader.

In a megacommunity, inclusiveness applies not only to participants but to those who stand to benefit. A megacommunity leader values solutions that will serve such diverse stakeholders as investors, union leaders, landowners, and neighbors. There is a working assumption that some solution exists that has some critical benefits for everyone. As John Schubert, chairman of the Commonwealth Bank of Australia, says, "The working out of what you want should not only be along the lines of a win for just you. A win for the other parts of the megacommunity is critical. Win-win-win for all parts! That is a prerequisite for success."

This prejudice toward inclusiveness manifests itself in many ways. Megacommunity leaders recognize that "win-win-win" solutions often require transforming the established practices and institutional barriers within their own organizations. For instance, they may need to institute new incentive structures, moving away from those that support individual advancement and toward valuing collaboration. The inclusive leader is also comfortable bridging the gap between internal and external constituencies.

Externally, this inclusive leader must realize there is a material—and psychological—benefit in having a real empathy for the constraints that each sector faces when attempting to operate in a globalized world. This inclusive leader must see new possibilities in new combinations of partners. Hence, a megacommunity leader must have a commitment to cross-sector engagement. In fact, we would go further and say that a good megacommunity leader needs actual tri-sector exposure.

TRI-SECTOR EXPOSURE

A great megacommunity leader needs to embrace, not just accept, the challenge of working in a larger, more complex sphere of influence. For this reason, the most successful leaders of the future may be those with career paths through all three sectors, either migrating through business, government, and the civil sectors during their careers, or serving on boards of organizations in other sectors.

Perhaps because the world demands it, we see an increasing number of "multiparty" or "integrative" leaders. Among them, we can count Richard Parsons, CEO of Time-Warner (who worked in the Gerald Ford administration and chaired the Apollo Theater Foundation), New York City Mayor Michael Bloomberg (former board member of Johns Hopkins University and founder and former CEO of Bloomberg L.P.), Renato Ruggiero (who served as Italy's minister of foreign affairs and World Trade Organization director-general, and is currently the chairman of Citigroup in Switzerland), and Henry M. Paulson, Jr. (who served as CEO of Goldman Sachs, chairman of the Board at the Nature Conservancy, and is currently the secretary of the Treasury for the U.S. government). We can happily say that they are only a few of an ever-increasing breed.

"One of the first things I tell our master in public affairs (MPA) students," says Anne-Marie Slaughter, dean of the Woodrow Wilson School of Public and International Affairs at Princeton University, "is that the career path in government has changed. Most of them will hold multiple jobs. They should think about the issues they're interested in—whether human rights, the environment, HIV/AIDS, energy, or geopolitics—and then pursue those issues in the private sector, the government sector, and the nonprofit sector, with maybe 10 or 15 years in each sector. Only if you move among them do you meet the people and learn the culture of all three sectors. And only then can you bring all three groups together to work on these issues."

This represents a significant change from the longstanding 30-year, one-job career of the typical government leader or business leader. "Now," says Dean Slaughter, "the U.S. State Department has a hard time getting the people they want because our best students don't want to work in one organization for 30 years, and they have spouses with careers, who aren't going to follow them around the world. Instead, you have people like one of my star students [who] worked under Richard Holbrooke at the U.S. Embassy to the United Nations. She then worked for Dow Jones, and is now the chief of operations at Human Rights Watch. Both government and nonprofits now want people like her, with experience, skills, and contacts in all three areas. This type of multifaceted career fits with the sort of dynamic movement that these students see for themselves, and with the networks that they want to build."[1]

We hear similar themes from the leaders themselves: people like Sakie Tachibana Fukushima, senior client partner and director of the executive search firm Korn/Ferry International. "In my own career," she states, "I started out in academia at Harvard University and then I went into journalism for one year. And then I was in a law practice for several years, and then government for five years, and now in business for the last 15 years. As a result, I am very much a strong believer in the importance of this multi-sector approach and of crossing these professional boundaries."

With a career path weaving through all three sectors, integrative leaders will have the opportunity to develop their business acumen, a keen sense of civic issues, and a balanced view of bureaucracy. They'll understand that tri-sector access is not only a matter of fairness. It is a matter of necessity. It is a source of dramatic advantage for themselves and their organizations.

A NON-IMPERIAL APPROACH

An integrative leader has a keen understanding that doing business (whatever your business) cannot be a solo show, driven by a single imperial personality. As we move further into the megacommunity age, "a deeper leadership is coming out," according to Elio Catania, former chairman and CEO of Italian Railways. "The Internet era swept away the stereotyped beautiful, aggressive leader, one who owned a sailing boat . . . who was very clever in buying and selling. They were the flowers, the butterflies of that very moment."

"We've all seen the sort of the hard-driving, take-no-prisoners, suffer-fools-not-at-all use of position power," says John Schubert. "That can be quite effective within a business organization. But within a megacommunity, that would be totally ineffective. You don't have a direct control over so many parts of it, so you need to be much more subtle. You just can't go and tell somebody to do something. Even in large organizations, that doesn't work all the time, as executives find out pretty quickly. You go and decide something and then three months later you find out—nothing's happened."

At first glance, this type of leadership seems more difficult than conventional "command and control" authoritarianism—exemplified by the style associated with military or corporate hierarchies. Leadership is very different in a networked environment. According to Ian Buchanan, "The big shift is from 'command and control' to 'coaching and persuading.'" The leader no longer pushes his or her people toward total competition, toward "taking no prisoners" or "dominating our market" at the expense of all others. The emphasis moves instead to strategic collaboration and permanent negotiation. Negotiation and facilitation assets must replace "positional" assets.

Each year, Booz Allen Hamilton studies trends in the tenure and succession rates of corporate chief executives around the world. The most recent study, published in *strategy + business* in 2007, suggests that the dominance of the imperial CEO is over. Instead, "inclusive leaders" are on the rise, and are "willing to engage in dialogue with investors, employees and government; to surround themselves with managers and advisors who complement their own capabilities; and to maintain transparency in their communications about financial results and compensation."[2]

As the Booz Allen Hamilton study suggests, nonimperial leaders are more accessible than the standard imperial leader. They must be seen as a player, contributing—and caring to contribute—to any significant ongoing debate. They cannot be isolated in a corporate ivory tower. As Fulvio Conti, CEO of Enel, has discovered, "I spend 60 percent of my time internally and 40 percent externally. Of this 40 percent, 50 percent is spent on what I call administrative politics, 50 percent to build relations and open dialogue, or megacommunity if you wish."

Of course, for any given senior leader operating within their own organization, positional authority will continue to apply. Megacommunity involvement doesn't mean abandoning your positional authority. It simply means that in some arenas, focused on particular complex problems, the corporation (or agency or organization) chooses to participate in a different way than its ordinary business practices. It chooses to assume that optimizing for a system larger than itself will further its own ends better than anything it could accomplish unilaterally. Thus, Enel chooses to believe that in siting and designing a green coal facility in the Veneto, all the constituents together, making a decision and implementing it together, will serve Enel's interests better than Enel could by acting alone. In other arenas, Enel will continue to act unilaterally.

Having made the decision to shift in this way in particular arenas, one challenge for leaders is clear: Can your behavior, and the behavior of people throughout your organization, match this new way of operating in this megacommunity sphere? Can you lead in new ways within the megacommunity on, say, Monday and Tuesday, while continuing to manage your organization in its old patterns on Wednesday, Thursday, and Friday? Or can you seek a form of leadership presence that will be adaptable to both circumstances? Different leaders will find their own ways of answering this question. Some will shift their styles; sometimes they will assign only the most predisposed leaders to work in the megacommunity. And some will find themselves and their subordinates changing their style in the old authoritarian organization as well.

NAVIGATION SKILLS (A LIGHT "TOUCH")

Remember: A megacommunity is largely uncharted territory. Megacommunity leadership is not a prescriptive kind of the strategy (that is, prescribing the details that others have to perform). The successful megacommunity leader is one who stimulates the need to collaborate, invents strategies that work for everybody, and keeps people motivated along those lines. Because this thing we call a megacommunity is more like a living organism than it is like an algorithm or a machine, megacommunity leadership is about navigation—keeping sight of a distant target while dealing with the ebbs and flows of daily activity.

Basically, we're talking about "touch." In a command and control situation, a leader has a strong and heavy touch. (In certain extreme cases, it might be viewed more as a fist.) In a megacommunity, the touch is lighter. It is a guiding touch, one that lets constituents self-discover.

This concept of "touch" is not just a matter of intensity. It's also a matter of scale. One could argue that a heavy touch has a limited reach. ("I'm in complete control of the ring nearest me.") On the other hand, a lighter touch has a broader reach, which is perfect for megacommunity maintenance.

Buchanan suggests that this "touch"-ing role might not fall to senior leaders so much as it does to members of their megacommunity team. He refers to this type of person as an "enabler."

"These enablers become a very critical part of the process," Buchanan says. "Some call them coaches, counselors, advisors. They are exceptionally unusual characters that are often invisible. You never read about them. You never see them in the organization chart. They're very crucial facilitators of leadership effectiveness in new complex, cohesive communities."

Over time, effective navigation will lead to proper alignment of the various people and organizations—so that they all come to hold a common sense of their vital interest and objectives, and so that they share more of their assumptions. "The whole alignment issue is immensely complex," says Buchanan. "You've got to very cleverly align all of the business institutional enablers, the KPIs [key performance indicators], the compensation system, to give people much more independence of action. You must give people complete clarity on how to align what they do day-to-day with the needs of the business and their bigger aspirations." According to Buchanan, a megacommunity leader needs to accept the challenge of creating "focal points, institutional focal points, which allow people to crystallize and then realize the shared vision."

There is a long-standing organizational change model that illuminates the most appropriate kind of navigational touch that a megacommunity leader can have. Imagine yourself trying to persuade others to tackle a complex project with you. Imagine, further, that you have a solution handy. It may not be the best possible solution, but it's one that you feel comfortable with. You know it's viable, and you know it can be accomplished. How do you communicate that proposal to others in a megacommunity?

The model suggests there are four possible approaches:

- Leaders can "tell" people what to do. They can say, "This is the path we're taking. I've considered it, I've decided, and we're going with it." This approach works in some hierarchical situations, though it has a disadvantage even there; it doesn't permit others to add their intelligence to the process. But it has very little impact in a megacommunity. Telling people what to do, when they have no hierarchical relationship to you and do not report to you, will not lead to any results at all. A few will comply, if they see it in their interest to do so. Some will ignore you politely. Others will not be polite.

- Leaders can "sell" people on what to do. Many leaders may be tempted to assume that their role in the megacommunity is to convince others of an appropriate objective. They may be highly skilled at this form of persuasion, having honed their technique on customers, constituents, donors, shareholders, and employees. But in a megacommunity setting, with its structure of open collegiality, selling can backfire. People who feel that they are being pressured will respond with opposition, and two or more leaders trying to sell slightly different ideas can polarize a group.

- Leaders can ask the megacommunity to "consult" with them. This approach sets up the megacommunity leader as, in effect, a client seeking help from the rest of the megacommunity. But that single leader still maintains control—or the perception of control—and all other participants are merely advisors. In other words, although the consulting approach seems far more participative than other approaches, it still represents a move toward unilateral decision-making, and in a full megacommunity, it will not survive.

- Finally, leaders can involve the megacommunity in an effort to "co-create" solutions. To be sure, it takes more skill and time to develop a solution this way; it involves genuine interest in the ideas and approaches that other people have to suggest. It probably involves synthesizing or combining those solutions in novel ways, making the final result more valuable than the sum of the parts.[3]

COMMUNICATION SKILLS

As the points above demonstrate, megacommunity leaders must have, or develop, superb communication skills. Communication skills—the ability to speak, negotiate, and listen effectively, in all the varied contexts of cross-sector collaboration and decision-making—may be the most important single set of personal assets possessed by a megacommunity leader.

Within their own organizations, megacommunity leaders have a huge communications job. They are continually called upon to make the megacommunity's case, to explain the larger priorities and galvanize support among their constituencies. A leader from the business sector, for example, may need to show shareholders the ways in which participating in a megacommunity will further their financial objectives, while the head of an NGO might need to demonstrate the benefits derived from being involved with organizations previously seen as the enemy. Meanwhile, the government liaison has the complex task of demonstrating clear value to the public interest and defusing suspicion that private interests will exploit the megacommunity relationships.

Integrative leaders must also be able to communicate within the megacommunity itself. They need to know something about the previous experiences of the constituent components, the worries of each of their constituencies, and how those worries might color the debates over particular issues. Leaders in a megacommunity understand how people will perceive, interpret, and act upon their messages.

TECHNOLOGICAL SAVVY

Along with communication skills—and not unconnected to them—megacommunity leadership requires a certain amount of technological competence (or, at least, the ability to draw upon the technical expertise in others). This type of technological know-how can be clustered into three overarching categories:

TOOLS

As demonstrated in chapter five, information technology can be applied by a megacommunity in many ways, through mapping, visualization, and other forms of communication via MySpace, Facebook, or variations. It can be helpful in reporting and organization. Leaders can also apply developments in such areas as transportation, biotechnology, and nano-technology. As Fulvio Conti recommends, "Push R&D to identify technologies that can be advanced not only in terms of costs but also in respect for the environment. That is a 'must' paradigm."

NEW MEDIA

A megacommunity leader should also be familiar with the kinds of new media that exist. Such technologies provide ways of not only communicating within the megacommunity but of getting one's message out to a wide group of people, via Web sites, wikis, written blogs, video blogs, texting, and all types of multi-media programming.

As part of its megacommunity outreach, Enel SpA, for example, is using a broad mix of media to reach out to each community and country in which it operates: Russia, the Balkans, Italy, Iberia, Central and South America, and the United States. Building on traditional TV and newspaper campaigns, Enel has established a distinguished presence on the Web via blogging. It has also launched a new magazine, *Oxygen*, that will be run as an independent journal and will feature the writing of experts, consumers, advocates, and clients on energy topics.

A good megacommunity leader recognizes that, thanks to the digital milieu of the Internet, media are evolving away from their classic role, defined here by no better expert than Dick Parsons, CEO of Time-Warner: "The media's role is to educate, but educate in the context of providing fair and balanced reporting on what is happening and, hopefully, thoughtful commentary in terms of insight as to why it's happening."

Along with monitoring the established media (TV, radio, newspapers), a thorough examination of relevant wikis and blogs will reveal how the megacommunity is being perceived. However, keep in mind that stories often go unchecked. Megacommunity leaders are wise to remain abreast of any false allegations that are being circulated in the media. Through the Internet, each individual has access to unprecedented amount of information, which is an overall good for the megacommunity. But divisive and irresponsible individuals also have access to the Internet soapbox, giving them the potential for upending the megacommunity's worthiest goals. New leaders will have to find ways to neutralize this negative impact.

SYSTEMS

In our discussion of network theory, we've begun to explore the concept of systems—groups of interdependent parts whose interrelationships can be understood together. Any network of people is a system as is any organization. But the idea of systems thinking is far broader, and embraces a wide variety of interrelated wholes, from biological systems (including the human body) to computer systems (including "artificial life" systems that simulate living entities) to the system of interrelated forces that produce the complex problem megacommunities are trying to solve.

For example, consider the many systemic forces that have contributed to the presence of HIV/AIDS in a region like India or Africa. There is the nature of the disease itself, and its transmission through some kinds of sexual activity. There are the economic factors, such as the prevalence of work that draws men away from their families, where they are more likely to consort with prostitutes; or the impact of HIV/AIDS on the working population of a region, and its effect in making it more difficult to recruit employees. There are social factors, such as the literacy rate (the more educated the people of a region are, the more likely they are to avoid risky behavior), or the prevalent belief in some parts of the world that sexual activity with a virgin will cure the disease. There are medical and technological factors, including the state of research on retroviral drugs and on HIV-resistant vaccines, and operational factors, such as the condition of roads and transportation logistics that might be needed to bring drugs to remote areas. There are factors that reinforce and exacerbate the disease—for example, the millions of orphans who lack a family structure in which to grow up. And there are factors that inherently limit the growth of the problem, such as the tendency of a community to draw together and change its behavior when a genuine crisis is perceived.

All of these factors affect each other, but the effectiveness of a solution depends on being able to regard those mutual effects with some sophistication: to be able to see what kinds of leverage will make most of the difference. For example, is it better for medical professionals to focus attention on treatment or prevention? What is the fastest and most effective way to shift attitudes that could prevent transmission of the virus? Answers to these questions, and many others, will depend on the leaders' understanding of the system involved, and particularly on those hard-to-see factors that turn out to have the greatest impact on human behavior. For instance, the cultural unwillingness of many people to discuss the disease, or the ways it is transmitted, is itself one of the leading factors in making it difficult to control.

Behind every major problem is a system to be understood. If you are concerned about emergency preparedness in the face of storms, you need to understand the systems of global climate change, because that may help determine how fast preventive technologies—such as new kinds of levees or storm protection—may need to be put in place. If you are dealing with the impact of globalization and wish to create a sustainable economy, then you are likely to find great value in charting the

flows of goods, energy, and capital into and out of your area, and the relationship of these flows to the cultural attitudes of people there.

There are many techniques for raising awareness of systems. As
we've shown, the strategic simulation approach, or "wargaming" as
some choose to call it, is, at its heart, exactly that—a way to simulate
the hidden factors of a system and help people recognize the implications of changes they make. The work of Jay Forrester, Peter Senge,
John Sterman, Jennifer Kemeny, and many others in the field of "system dynamics" (that is, the study of the behavior of complex systems)
has led to a body of practices for helping model and talk about systemic forces. Economics itself is a form of systems study, particularly
those branches of economics, like behavioral economics and game theory analysis, that incorporate the study of human behavior. And there
is yet another body of work on systems understanding emerging from
cybernetics. Different methods will be valuable to different megacommunity leaders, but they all have the virtue of raising awareness of systems—showing people not just how to change the parts of a system,
but to affect the ways in which the parts work together. That's the definition of systems thinking.

As someone who understands networks, the megacommunity
leader will not only create the necessary understanding of linkages for
him or herself, but also encourage other players to do the same. This is
not going to be easy for a leader accustomed to having all the answers. It
is far more effective to involve people in an exercise in which they come
to recognize the answers for themselves, and to begin their own proto-

typing of solutions, than to simply hold a lecture and tell people what to do. The more people have a chance to talk about the ramifications of the system they're in, and the possible solutions, the more likely they are to collectively find an innovative set of ways to get out from under.

One of your jobs as a navigator, meanwhile, is to keep the group on track, moving forward on an emerging path. Understanding the systemic nature of the megacommunity's problem is just a first step. It's easy to stop there. But that's just the beginning of the process. A variety of questions need to be answered. What are the things that absolutely have to be changed? What elements of the system should be left alone—or, at the very least, changed with great care? What should megacommunity leaders do to change them? Where's the leverage—the greatest results for the least cost and effort? How can leaders and their fellow participants in the megacommunity scope out the unintended consequences?

All these questions get answered over time, as you steep yourself in systems thinking, and as you apply your own reflective ability to the results of the megacommunity's experiments. You must be aware that you are not just understanding the system, but acting to change it. Even your observations will have the effect of change: The Heisenberg theory, which describes the fact that observers in quantum physics change the nature of the phenomena they observe, seems to be true in many social systems, including megacommunities. If a megacommunity triggers massive interactions, as a healthy megacommunity surely will, you are "literally looking at a network," to quote Pablo de la Flor.

ADAPTABILITY

As George Yong-Boon Yeo suggests, "You have to be a student first." Adaptability—or openness to influence—is the hallmark of a good megacommunity leader.

A megacommunity leader is intellectually curious about the world and their organization's place in it. Understanding the megacommunity's other constituents means embracing the broad range of cultural backgrounds and attitudes (including historical backgrounds and their implications) within the region or domain of interest.

But a good megacommunity leader should be a student of sustainable globalization. This in itself requires openness to different peoples' understanding: to recognize the ways in which the relevant economic and political realities are changing, and how such changes have altered the roles of and demands on leaders in the area. In this regard, it is very valuable for megacommunity leaders to be well-traveled. This may not mean literally traveling to far-flung places, but, rather, turning a travelers' eye on the dynamics of your local situation. Good leaders need to know what's going on in the world.

"I am convinced," says Fulvio Conti, "that a manager needs to be a person that dispels 'culture' in its broad sense, to create value. By culture, I mean combining the scientific notions with humanism, being a 'citizen of the world.' If you want to be able to detect, sense and manage the changes around you, the leader's view should not be confined to the role in the specific industry or sector in which he or she operates. The leader needs to be like a sponge that absorbs trends, changes, stimuli that arise from and around his operating environment—including other geographies."

Anne-Marie Slaughter adds, "If you're comfortable with letting your perspective evolve, then you can be much more effective leading a network. [Being a network-oriented leader] is risky, but only if you, as a leader, see yourself as an autonomous agent who has charted a course and doesn't want to be deflected."

As a state of mind, adaptability is not just the willingness to absorb and aggregate information. Openminded, adaptable leaders also know how to synthesize their insight—and act upon it. In this regard, a good megacommunity leader is a "continuous adopter": trying out new ideas in limited ways, monitoring the changes they produce, and then applying them more generally.

THE TALENT TO FOSTER TALENT

A megacommunity leader will not be able to necessarily hire a staff that has succeeded in this type of work before, because such work hasn't been done as prolifically as it will—or should—be in the future. As a result, a megacommunity leader has to be a good team and talent builder, drawing out qualities and capabilities that people didn't know they had until they begin to use them. As Ken Chenault, CEO of American Express, told us: "If globalization is going to bring about a more enlightened age, we're going to have to work—whether it's in NGOs, governments or corporations—to think more consciously about how we train and develop leaders to deal with these issues."

Great megacommunity leaders are continually engaged in fostering and developing human capital. As Conti notes, "We have to be able to create multicultural leaders that are ready to operate in symbiosis with the environment. This is of paramount importance, in order to forge the depth of the values on which megacommunity platforms are then created."

We suspect that, over time, megacommunities themselves will become a prime breeding ground for training integrated leaders with multi-sector experience. Leaders can further this kind of on-the-job training in many ways, through the definition of discrete tasks, complete with feedback sessions in which experience is shared, or through "seconding" programs (also known as "hostage exchange"), whereby employees are given the chance to work in other sectors or in different organizations within their own sector. A hostage exchange program is a particularly direct way of exposing potential new leaders to the needs of the other players in the megacommunity, and helps stronger bonds grow between organizational elements. In fact, this concept goes back to the Middle Ages. Known as "fostering," it was used by warring factions to keep peace and build understanding.

A value-based leadership approach also helps in the "war for talent." As articulated by Chenault, "If you're not focused—irrespective of whether you operate in a range of markets—in getting some of the best people around the world, and in fact creating an environment where they feel they can really prosper, where they're going to be respected, you will clearly lose out in a major way in the marketplace." There are already signs that megacommunities represent a desirable environment for the best and the brightest new recruits.

According to Ian Buchanan, "A lot of business leaders I work with are a bit puzzled by how to engage the new generations of workers. When I left Wharton in '72, the first questions I asked [potential employers] were: When will I be a partner? And how much will I then make? We don't get asked that anymore. It's: What are you doing to impact the community around you? What can I do to help achieve the bigger impact on society that's important to me within the institutional structure? So, over the last decade, many organizations have set up very active community service groups, which are owned and run by the staff. This empowers your staff not just within the confines of your own institution but—as you crystallize what's important to them—it reaches out to other institutions."

This sounds to us like the seeds of megacommunity.

PRESENCE AND PASSION

Even though the era of the "beautiful, aggressive," "take-no-prisoners" leader may be waning, personal characteristics still determine an individual's leadership potential. A megacommunity leader must have a strong, centered presence. There has to be an authenticity to the megacommunity leader, some human-to-human resonance. Reading accounts of megacommunities, one imagines that an ideal leader has to be self-assured but humble, generous as opposed to cynical. Insight, patience, resolve, creativity, and determination all come it play, as well as a heightened sense of empathy, an ability to put oneself in someone else's shoes. Of course, no human being qualifies on every single one of these counts. But there is one primary personal quality that a megacommunity leader must have.

That single element is passion. After all, a megacommunity does not become truly viable until leaders make it part of their personal agenda. Through passion and conviction, a leader becomes inspirational. Passion is contagious. And passion is the hallmark of an honest broker. Good megacommunity leaders must know how to use their passion to drive issues from the realm of personal interest to institutional commitment. Passion without action won't get you much. And the opposite is also true. As Raj Kondur, founder and CEO of Nirvana Business Solutions, points out, "Process without passion is bureaucracy."

LONG-TERM THINKING

Last but not least, we come back to our favorite word, the one with which we began this book: sustainability. A megacommunity leader must be oriented toward the sustainable. Great megacommunity leaders are always looking far ahead. They should be working toward a platform that is strong on underlying values (and value creation) that might be exported. He or she should always be horizon-scanning for things that can derail the megacommunity. And this leader should not be fearful of embracing far-flung, sometimes abstract goals such as social peace and cohesion. Members from all three sectors must be able to, as Robert Switz of ADC Telecommunications, Inc., says, "Stay the course and make a long, long, long-term unwavering commitment."

A megacommunity leader is often ahead of the curve. Long-term thinking leads to foresight, and can make it easier to predict the right moves in advance, to educate others and prevent problems before they occur. Megacommunity leaders know that pre-set answers are not going to cut it. They are accustomed to thoughtful trial-and-error. And they embrace the pragmatic and new solutions that few others can see.

As Anne-Marie Slaughter recalled, "I recently heard a senior executive of a major engineering firm say, 'We don't plan anymore.' The pace of change was accelerating so fast, he said, that the best they could do was react faster than everybody else. So why bother planning? You see what's coming down the pike and you go with it."

A great megacommunity leader is someone who sets things up to endure. To ensure long-term success, a megacommunity leader must also be extremely thoughtful regarding the notion of succession. Senior leaders who really believe in the megacommunity have a responsibility to deeply integrate those beliefs into their organizations, so that when they are gone those beliefs continue to function.

This kind of thinking may seem antithetical in a world in which CEO tenures are said to be growing shorter. But the Booz Allen CEO succession study found increasing stability in the years from 2004 to 2006, which "contrasts with the previous decade's rapid increases in both turnover and forced turnover."[4] Meanwhile, many of the leaders we interviewed stressed the need for long-term planning, to get beyond short-term thinking and the laser-like focus on quarterly results.

According to Craig Middleton, vice chairman of Young and Rubicam Brands, "The kinds of issues that link us as global citizens are not along the short-term. They're the long-term things. Being able to work with multiple horizons is what separates the successful CEO from the one who's not. Particularly if the successful CEO is able to both make money for their shareholders and make contributions to developing Third World economies. That isn't their job; but if they do it in the fall-out of doing the rest of their job correctly, then they've served everyone well. And they'll realize that they've been balancing this kind of thing all the time."

Marjorie Yang, chairwoman and CEO of Esquel Group, says: "I believe that there are many good CEOs who are very mature. One of the things that this group of CEOs is saying is 'Look, we have to tell the analysts to stop evaluating companies with such myopic views.' If you're only looking at quarterly results, you're driving the wrong behavior. Let us form, as a group, to put the pressure back on the analysts. They are very short-sighted. Now, the format must be changed, so companies must be judged based upon the long-term visions and values."

"Of course, you have to be able to demonstrate value creation along the way," says Conti, "but with, again, a long-term vision. Those in my position that try to maximize the short-term according to their three-year term mandate, make a mistake. And they run the risk of not being reappointed."

In many ways, thinking in the long-term or the short-term is an artificial choice. Leaders do not have to lose all their focus on short-term benefits in favor of long-term planning. They can do both. And given its scaling capabilities, a megacommunity is the perfect context for this kind of dual track. With good leadership, we're confident that the mega-community can achieve both short-term and long-term success.

We offer these ten elements of megacommunity leadership in full knowledge that some leaders in some industries have not yet been touched by megacommunity phenomena. But in our view, we will all be touched by it eventually. The megacommunity concept may well help to reshape industrial relations within society in the years to come. It may well influence the social construct and the social contract on which our quality of living—and our very lives—are based.

Even in the megacommunity context, there will still be winners. But the notion of who's on your team and what winning means is, in fact, changing. Megacommunity involvement teaches you to respect the value of the network and allows you to optimize that value. In this way, we feel that the megacommunity concept is the answer to—and the perfect reflection of—so many of the changes brought about by globalization in particular. In the most direct terms, a growing disparity in thought and a growing fragmentation across sectors must be met by a growing determination to come together in a sustainable way. Ultimately, this is the challenge. And it's a challenge that megacommunities meet head-on.

AFTERWORD

A MEGACOMMUNITY SUCCESS STORY

"If you think of the things that need to happen for the world to continue to improve or, actually, not get worse, then they all involve megacommunities and megacommunity decisions. And the decisions that can be made in single communities aren't the critical ones that we're facing. The critical decisions and directions that the world is facing all involve megacommunities."

—John Schubert, chairman of the
Commonwealth Bank of Australia
and chair of the
Great Barrier Reef Foundation

Throughout this book, we have been following the story of Enel SpA—its discovery of the need for megacommunity when it experienced the shutdown of a project in Brindisi, Italy, and its subsequent deployment of megacommunity ideas in the Italian region of the Veneto. In closing this book, we would like to take a closer look at the nature of their experiences in megacommunity, to illustrate the across-the-board positive effect—on Enel—of putting megacommunity ideas into action. The story of Enel in the Veneto clearly illustrates the benefits to a specific player within a megacommunity, and the ample benefits that flow to those who work out ways to balance tensions between sectors (whether those tensions manifest as conflicting action plans, profit goals, or points of view).

In 2005, Enel decided to move toward overhauling power-generating plants along the Po River in the Veneto so that they could burn what is referred to as "green coal," which produces less environmentally damaging effects when burned because of advanced treatment technologies. But Enel realized that this positive benefit did not guarantee acceptance and that there were specific local dimensions to any plan for overhauling power plants in a specific region. The local communities involved were sure to have all sorts of valid concerns, ranging from health and safety to jobs, and so forth. And, as Enel learned in Brindisi, there were certain key local constituencies—such as the media and environmental groups— that would surely not allow themselves to be ignored. In fact, their cooperation might add extra benefit in insights and capabilities all around.

Surely, the issue of overhauling plants affected all three sectors; there would be an overlap of vital interests among the sectors and a need for convergence over how to best approach the issue. In essence, this issue of overhauling plants in the Veneto had all the features of a highly complex megacommunity problem. Enel came to the conclusion that, if they were not mindful of all the constituencies involved, their desire to overhaul the area's power plants could quickly lead to a set of cascading and unintended consequences, multiplying costs and risks— perhaps going so far as to put a halt to the project. In the language of a megacommunity, Enel saw the real danger associated with trying to maximize their position in this important and complicated undertaking. Isolated from the other stakeholders in the issue and uninformed by their perspectives, Enel could have chosen an approach that, on its surface, would have seemed to meet its own needs. And in this type of situation, an admonition of H. L. Mencken comes to mind: "For every complex problem, there is an answer that is clear, simple, and wrong."

Instead of falling into the maximizing trap, Enel leaders, working with Booz Allen, began to explore the megacommunity mindset by first adopting an attitude of openness and flexibility, and then converting those attitudes into action.

In a very deliberate and conscious manner, Enel decided to initiate a megacommunity around the development project in the Veneto. But, they asked themselves, what did this mean in terms of behavior? To begin the process, what steps should they immediately take? What kind of systemized approach might be useful in the long run? And perhaps most important, and vexing, who should take the first steps?

From the outset, Enel seemed to be the best organization to successfully convene the megacommunity. They clearly understood their own vital interests and could articulate them; they saw the value of the megacommunity approach, and in fact had seen the ineffectual nature of other alternatives (à la Brindisi); and they had the standing, resources, and corporate culture to pull it off. Enel realized that optimizing creates more value than maximizing, and, as more often than not in this industry, maximization leads to reduced shareholder value over the longer term.

As an initial step, Enel decided to embrace two important tasks: informing and educating. They felt they had to reach beyond the boundaries of their own company to explain how addressing infrastructure concerns—such as those represented by their plans in the Veneto—were instrumental to a country that wished to compete, create jobs, and remain a leader on a global scale in the decades to come. To accomplish their goal, Enel moved out on several fronts at once.

On the local front, Enel began to identify and map local groups along a sophisticated matrix (previously illustrated in chapter four) that allowed the company to develop an understanding of the "insights" of each of the effected constituencies. Using what we call a full stakeholder mapping, Enel began a process of ranking these constituencies in relevance. Enel soon realized that certain conflicts are embedded and cannot be avoided. Drawing information from the matrix, they forecast which conflicts had priority, in the hopes of avoiding a negative domino effect. In honest broker fashion, keeping their eye on the danger of co-opting another constituency's specific issues, Enel provided the information and data it had gathered to the most influential stakeholders, focusing on the issues it had previously identified through various open-source techniques. By showing their interest in addressing the local dimension, Enel took a major step toward creating consensus—a consensus that meant that they themselves would have to think more carefully about certain aspects of their plans. As in any thorough initiation process, Enel's efforts also facilitated the jobs of those in the other sectors (such as the central government), by aligning objectives and working toward optimizing the outcome. All their actions showed signs of paving the way for a faster resolution of the issues at stake—a natural and essential benefit of megacommunity.

In many ways, Enel in the Veneto is the purest type of megacommunity situation because it has so many potential repercussions. Enel saw the need to look beyond the boundaries of the Veneto, to reach out along international and regional lines. They felt it was important to provide the widest possible range of opinion-makers (the media, the EU commission, academia, nationally-based activists) with a clear vision and action plan that explained the entire picture in all its dimensions— not only along the lines of Enel's strict and immediate interests, but along the lines of the megacommunity writ large.

Through his external communications, Enel CEO Fulvio Conti moved toward a profile that is closer to that of an integrative leader than a traditional chief executive. By calling for a strategy and an agenda that looks well beyond the atomized interests of each of the current players scattered unevenly and inefficiently across the European landscape, Conti changed the frame of reference of all those engaged.

In a *Financial Times* column on November 17, 2006, Conti states, "Europe needs to act as one on energy supply ... As legislation is drafted for implementation next year, there is an urgent need for politicians to recognize that energy is a challenge for the whole of Europe. Energy companies have their important role to play in building a single market but as European citizens we all have the opportunity to safeguard our future and we must not miss it . . . 65 percent of energy is imported and this is expected to rise to more than 80 percent in 20 years . . . This is not a challenge that can be dealt with effectively by 27 independent micro-markets." Demonstrating the scalability of the megacommunity approach, Conti suggests the development of a more regionally-oriented megacommunity, a European energy megacommunity that can work together as a single entity. He writes that "sustainable energy development must also be directed by Europe. Think of the reduced costs of shared research and development in renewable energy technologies. Think of what could be achieved if the same efficiency standards were applied across Europe. The International Energy Agency has calculated that by 2050 energy-efficient technologies could bring emissions back to 2000 levels." In an ultimate leap in scale, Conti clearly articulated his view of a megacommunity that can produce locally, regionally, and globally.

As Enel discovered, involvement in a megacommunity also leads to extremely beneficial evolutions within an organization. Enel has had to adapt internally. Those within Enel who are initiating and involved in this megacommunity need to be supported by its organization, human resources, processes, and technology if they wish to achieve their goal. Enel has reengineered itself to comply with this challenge. They have created a suite of new management (including a "megacommunity manager"). They have readjusted their human resources stock of capabilities. They have expanded their communication strategy and execution along traditional, as well as new media. A new executive management "dashboard" has been created that allows swift communication and dialogue between individual members of the megacommunity and Enel's CEO and top management within the region. This tool provides management with timely sensing and awareness information. As a result, the company will be more effective in engaging, nurturing, and sustaining megacommunity, and also in supporting any efforts, including CEO efforts, in this regard.

To the company's benefit, social issues have become a strategic item on Enel's general agenda. As proof, a recent internal Enel climate survey with its 90,000 employees across the world had a stunning feedback of close to 60,000 responses. Moreover, Enel has linked issues that are voiced at the local level with broader international debates and dialogue, always striving to clarify the expanding agenda in a hyper-reactive, technology-intensive environment—realizing that their specific issues in the Veneto link to perhaps the most hotly debated issue of this century: global climate change.

Moreover, Enel's experience in megacommunity has provided the company with a relevant template as it becomes a truly global player with its October 2007 acquisition of Endesa, the largest electric utility company in Spain. Against this background (and in line with its megacommunity role), Enel has joined forces with Harvard University to create the Enel Endowment for Environmental Economics, a cross-school chair that draws upon the expertise of the ten schools within Harvard. With the leadership and prestige of Harvard University behind it, Enel will act as a participant in the environmental community, providing position papers, option assessments, and action plans in respect to some of our most challenging environmental issues—issues ranging from the Post Kyoto Protocol to energy security to the issue of carbon management on a global scale. This approach is further reinforced by Enel's launch of *Oxygen*—a quarterly magazine designed to promote independent view points from political, business, and civil society opinion leaders. From one point of view, Enel's efforts can be seen as connecting the man on the street in Veneto with the international community of scientists that are addressing his concerns, his need for a better life, and his desire to preserve the environment. This binding of local and global concerns is one of the major benefits of megacommunity thinking and action—and that can only bode well for the sustainability of globalization and for the planet.

Ultimately, Enel's concerto of vision, techniques, and actions has led to an articulated and proactive megacommunity in the Veneto, and to the proposal of a potential European environmental megacommunity. It has also had a profound effect on how Enel itself is perceived. Progressively, there is a shared consensus about the validity of Enel's vision for the future, and its standing as an environmentally conscience leader. In the world community, Enel is increasingly perceived as a positive player striving for a better world. Following an older paradigm, this change in stature may have been the main reason for the actions taken by a company. But in a megacommunity, this is only a side benefit (albeit an extremely desirable side benefit), and only one example of the cascading benefits to be found in adopting the megacommunity mindset.

All the benefits that Enel has accrued are exactly in line with our vision of megacommunity. We view megacommunity as an organic evolution in the way the world operates, and we project that it can lead to a wide array of intended and unintended benefits, from the most pragmatic (wealth creation) to the most expansive (a new social contract for the new millennium). And we can only assume that it prefigures further organic changes in the future—as one local megacommunity becomes the first pinpoint in a constellation of megacommunities (much like the

Harlem Initiative inspired small business environments in many other cities), or as a local megacommunity leaps in scale to become a global megacommunity (much like Enel's Veneto experience is already seeding a Europe-wide reaction).

The megacommunity way is a response to a growing complexity we all see and feel, of which globalization is only a part, albeit an important part. It calls for the recognition and engagement of a much larger sphere of interest, and an adaptation of goals that are ongoing and mutable over time. Keeping all the elements of a megacommunity in view is an enormous challenge. Unlike the elegant, self-managed networks of nature, mankind has built an immense amount of complexity into the networks we use everyday, and we have not managed them in an effective way. A new degree of connectedness between the diverse component parts is essential, as well as a new set of institutional capabilities, ones that foster coordination, understanding, and education. But the road to megacommunity does not have to be an endlessly complicated one. As the Enel example shows, if you have people practicing the right activities, their day-to-day experiences will be self-reinforcing. As in any system, if you have the properties set correctly, these properties tend to seed one another.

We believe that the concept of megacommunity will have a profound effect on the way we see, and function in, the new world. As part of a megacommunity, all three sectors—government, business, and the civil society—are in an excellent position to have a real and lasting effect on large and complex problems. It may seem that, joined together, the three sectors would make any situation more complex. But in fact, when designed and managed correctly, a megacommunity reduces complexity—as it has in Harlem, the Veneto, the Great Barrier Reef, and elsewhere. More and more leaders now seem to be aware of this. When megacommunities fail to form, it's not from lack of desire, but from lack of capability. Will leaders be able to take up the megacommunity challenge and produce the results that the world needs? Experience suggests that they can and we believe they will.

GLOSSARY

Business Process Reengineering A management science approach designed to improve. The efficiency and effectiveness of the processes that support organizations (both internal and external processes).

Butterfly Effect The concept that sensitivity to "initial conditions" creates a situation in which events in one area of a network can cause major and unpredictable responses in other parts of the network. The uncertainty arises from the minute variations in measured values between each set part of the network. In the context of weather, the concept refers to the idea that if a butterfly flaps its wings in a certain part of the world, it can make a difference in whether or not a storm arises on the other side of the world.

Cause and Effect A situation of predictable behavior within a system; an if–then relationship usually based on previous experience.

Civil Society One of three global sectors. It represents a collection of nongovernmental organizations (NGOs) and intermediary institutions such as professional associations, religious groups, labor unions, and citizen advocacy organizations. It is also known as the "nonprofit world" and the "third sector," and is quite distinct from government and business.

Command and Control A hierarchical decision support structure (in which information flows up the chain and decisions flow down) composed of self-contained modules (e.g., platoons, companies, battalions in the military) that interact with the outside as a single object.

Complex System A system whose behavior emerges from the interaction among many independent actors (agents) without any central control mechanism or strategy.

Control-Free Zone A conceptual part of a network in which control mechanisms are ineffective.

Convergence A representation of common ground between objectives that manifests in a commitment toward mutual action.

Cross-Organizational Structures A configuration of organizations from different global sectors built upon a set of protocols and organizing principles that bring a degree of order to the relationships to provide an operating environment conducive to the application of "dynamic tension."

Dynamic Tension The way, in a healthy megacommunity, the three sectors maintain balance by "pushing" and "pulling" at each other according to their respective forms of influence.

Geocomplexity   A category of global issues in which social, political, military, and economic activities interact as a complex system and in which the dynamic nature of the issues make top–down, command-and-control, and reductionist management methods ineffective. Instead, geocomplexity calls for innovative, integrated, and holistic management approaches.

Global Dynamics   The term used to describe a new way of thinking about a wide variety of global challenges that recognizes that there are a host of factors—complexity, politics, economics, culture, technology, demographics, environmental—that influence how global issues are identified, debated, and addressed. Examining these challenges through the Global Dynamics lens reveals the need for mutual leadership, activities that bring decision-makers from business, government, and civil-sector institutions together to collaborate.

Global Sectors   An aggregation of organizations and entities operating globally that are categorized by their primary focus area: business, the government, or civil society. Taken together, they are also known as *Tri-Sector.*

Governance   The administrative processes and related systems by which an organization operates.

Graph   A collection of nodes (vertices) and a collection of links (edges) that connect pairs of nodes. A graph may be undirected, meaning that there is no distinction between the two nodes associated with each link, or its links may be directed from one node to another.

Graph Theory   The study of graphs; mathematical structures used to model the relations between objects in an interconnected structure.

High-Order Language   In functional programming, higher-order languages support higher-order functions and allow the functions to be part of larger data structures (a higher-order function accepts functions as arguments and is able to return a function as its result).

Hub   A specialized node in a network that connects to several other nodes (i.e., it has a high number of linkages into and out of it).

Initiator   An entity that takes the lead in moving a megacommunity from its latent stage to an active state.

Integrative Leader   Leader with career experience in all three sectors, either migrating through business, government, and the civil sectors during their careers, or serving on the boards of organizations in various sectors.

Link   An interconnecting mechanism between two or more nodes in a network for the purpose of transmitting and receiving information, material, and other commodities.

Maximize   To increase to the greatest possible amount or degree.

Megacommunity   A collaborative socioeconomic environment in which business, government, and civil society interact according to their common interests, while maintaining their unique priorities.

Network   A collection of vertices or "nodes" and a collection of links that connect pairs of nodes.

Network Analysis   The study of complex, interconnected groups or systems comprised of nodes and links using the elements graph theory.

Network Capital   The value of the investment in relationships and connections associated with one's social network in a megacommunity.

Node   An originating or terminating point of exchange in a network.

Open Networks   Networks that can be easily expanded or scaled back because they do not have any built-in barrier for entry to new participants.

Open Source Analysis   Examination and assessment of information to support decision making, from sources that are publicly available and not gathered through any clandestine or illegal methods.

Optimize   To make as effective, perfect, or useful as possible. In mathematics, to determine the maximum or minimum values of a specified function that is subject to certain constraints.

Overlapping Vital Interest   The combination of a shared issue with a sense of shared impact among the members of a megacommunity.

Pattern Study   A structured examination of data and indicators (i.e., patterns) based on either *a priori* knowledge or on statistical information extracted from the patterns to support decision making.

Prisoner's Dilemma   A teaching type of game in which two players may each "cooperate" with or "defect" (i.e., betray) the other player. In this game, the only concern of each individual player ("prisoner") is maximizing his/her own payoff, without any concern for the other player's payoff.

Private Sector   One of three global sectors. It represents a collection of enterprises operating within the economy that is both run for profit and is not controlled by the state.

Public Sector   One of three global sectors. It represents a collection of entities that are part of the economic and administrative life that deals with the delivery of goods and services by and for the government, whether national, regional, local, or municipal.

Rule of Law   A fundamental principle that governmental authority can be considered legitimate when it is exercised in accordance with written, publicly disclosed laws adopted and enforced in accordance with well-understood procedure. This principle sets a "level playing field" for organizations and individuals operating within the realm of control of governmental authority.

Scale-Free Network   A specific kind of network in which the distribution of connectivity is extremely uneven. In scale-free networks, some nodes act as "very connected" hubs using a power-law distribution. The term "scale-free" was first coined by physicist Albert-László Barabási and his colleagues at the University of Notre Dame.

Simple System   A system whose behavior is determined by a central control mechanism and strategy.

Stakeholder   Any entity or organization that can be positively or negatively impacted by, or cause an impact to, the course of action taken by a member of the megacommunity.

Stakeholder Analysis   An analysis that aims to identify the stakeholders upon whom an initiative depends for its success and/or that are affected by the results of the initiative.

Strong-tie   In a network, the link between two nodes that is based on a strong and vibrant, ongoing relationship—a situation in which the individuals have a high amount of contact.

Swarm Intelligence   A behavioral science technique based around the study of collective behavior in decentralized, self-organized systems. The term was introduced by Gerardo Beni and Jing Wang in 1989, in the context of cellular robotic systems.

System   An aggregate whose performance results from the interaction of its two or more component parts.

System Dynamics   An element of systems theory used as a way of understanding the dynamic behavior of complex systems. It recognizes that the structure of any system—the interconnected nodes and the links—is a major contributor in determining the behavior of the system. System dynamics was created during the mid-1950s by Professor Jay W. Forrester of the Massachusetts Institute of Technology.

Systems Thinking   An approach to integration that is based on the belief that the component parts of a system will act differently when isolated from the system's environment or other parts of the system.

Tipping Point   A point in the behavior of a system (the angle of repose) at which the event of a previously rare phenomenon becomes much more common. Mathematically, the angle of repose is a kind of inflection point. The phrase has expanded over time to take on a much broader meaning, and has been applied in many fields, from economics to epidemiology. It is also used to describe a phase transition in physics or the propagation of populations in an unbalanced ecosystem.

Total Quality Management   A management strategy aimed at embedding awareness of quality in all organizational processes.

Transitive   A type of relationship among nodes in a network, where if a relation exists between "a" and "b" and between "b" and "c," then it must also exist between "a" and "c."

Tri-Sector Engagement   When all three global sectors act in concert to address an issue of mutual concern or interest.

Value Chain   A management tool that categorizes the generic value-adding activities of an organization using "primary activities" (e.g., inbound logistics, operations/production, outbound logistics, marketing and sales, and services/maintenance) and "support activities" including administrative infrastructure management, human resource management, R&D, and procurement.

Value Network   Representations of complex combinations of value chains (i.e., sets of social and technical resources that work together through relationships to create economic value) where the value can take the form of knowledge, intelligence, a product (business), services, innovation, or social good. Examples of business value networks are research, development, design, production, marketing, sales, organizational learning, procurement, and distribution (business).

Visualization   Any technique for creating images, diagrams, or animations to communicate any message, as well as with the presentation of large quantities of data to aid cognition, hypotheses building, and reasoning.

Vital Interest   An interest (or issue) that is so central to the mission / objective / goals of an organization, enterprise, or entity that serious harm can happen unless strong measures are taken.

Wargame   A learning exercise or approach that provides participants with a way to simulate the hidden factors of a system and help them recognize the implications of the changes they make.

Washington Consensus   A phrase coined by John Williamson in the late 1980s to describe a set of ten specific economic policy prescriptions that were considered to constitute a "standard" reform package promoted for crisis-wracked countries by Washington-based institutions such as the International Monetary Fund, World Bank, and the U.S. Treasury Department. The term "Washington Consensus" has since acquired a secondary connotation, being used to describe a less-precisely stipulated gamut of policies, broadly associated with expanding the role of market forces and constraining the role of the state.

Weak-tie   In a network, the link between two nodes that is not based on a strong and vibrant, ongoing relationship—a situation in which the individuals do not have regular contact.

Zero-Sum Game   A situation in which a participant's gain or loss is exactly balanced by the losses or gains of the other participant(s). It is so named because when the total gains of the participants are added up, and the total losses are subtracted, they will sum to zero.

ACKNOWLEDGMENTS

G iven the central theme of this book—that by creating a community of concerned, committed participants, great things can (and will) happen—we feel it is very important to call attention to the many people who took the time to talk about ideas, read drafts, and advise us in ways that made a tremendous difference to the quality and value of *Megacommunities*.

While the book you are reading is made up of our words, more than a few people have had a share in rearranging, reordering, and generally improving them. First and foremost, Larry Frascella, who helped us remember more of our college English classes than we ever thought we could, and for his inestimable assistance in structuring this book. Larry is a consummate professional, without whom we would have struggled mightily to produce *Megacommunities*. In addition, our colleague Art Kleiner has been an invaluable addition to the team. Art's insight and knowledge added significantly to the content of the book, and his editorial expertise has improved the book in too many ways to even begin to list here.

Mike Delurey has been with the project from the beginning, and has served as the hub in our network of activity. We drew heavily on his original work in communities of shared mission and social risk in developing the megacommunity concept. His knowledge of networks and complex systems also helped to shape the theories presented here, and his dedication to the project kept us moving.

The overwhelming task of organizing, coordinating, scheduling, and managing the tasks associated with the book has been borne primarily by two outstanding consultants with our firm—Elizabeth Kytle and Claire Superfine. We cannot say enough about their tireless work driving the project, and how much we truly appreciate their efforts. In addition to Beth and Claire, we had stellar research and review support from Denis Cosgrove, Kathy Hebert, Brendan Schreiber, Bob Leaton, Cynthia Sibley, Mike Magoon, Margaret Lidstone, Judith Hegedus, Komal Bazaz Smith, James Bryant, Emily Ohland, and Joe Babiec.

No effort of this scale can be accomplished without superior administrative support. We were fortunate to have a fantastic team of professionals supporting us with such things as scheduling, trip organization, coordinating reviews, mass mailings, and clearing calendar time to find time to write. Our sincere appreciation goes to Paola Iappelli, Bernadette DaCruz, Cathy Saunders, Robin Souder, Liz Sapienza, Christine Iurato, and Dana Warner for all their help throughout this journey. A special thanks to Porter Hovey for her efforts in finding space in New York for us—never an easy task!

Transcriptions of the conversations with leaders from across the globe were a key part of this books' research. Sharon Lee Harkey handled our transcriptions wonderfully, despite the ongoing challenges of technology and tight deadlines.

We would like to single out several people for the time they spent guiding us through the journey to create *Megacommunities:* James Nicholson, former U.S. ambassador to the Holy See and later U.S. Secretary for Verterans Affairs, for introducing us to State of Vatican leadership to get their view on globalization. The Honorable Aziz Mekouar, Moroccan ambassador to the United States, for setting up the interview with Moroccan Prime Minister Driss Jettou. Henry Kissinger, for his initial advice and counseling on the trajectories that it was certainly worthwhile following. Yotaro Kobayashi, Fuji Xerox president and former Booz Allen Hamilton Global Advisory Board member, whose assistance was crucial to setting up the interviews in Japan. Our colleague Ed Tse, vice president and managing director of Greater China, whose leadership and reputation allowed us to dialogue with Chinese leaders. Fedele Confalonieri, Mediaset chairman and member of the Booz Allen Hamilton European Advisory Board, who was instrumental in helping us interview key Italian leaders. Richard H. K. Vietor, the Senator John Heinz professor of Environmental Management at the Harvard Graduate School of Business Administration. Honorable Gaetano Quagliariello, senator of the Italian Republic for setting up the interview with José María Aznar, former Spanish prime minister. Anusha Srinivasan, Booz Allen Hamilton associate in our New York office, for introducing us to the Indian leadership during a forum on India at HBS in 2004. Didier Pineau Valencienne, chairman of Booz Allen Hamilton's European Advisory Board, for his great mentorship over this year and passion for the "rare factor." Giosetta Capriati, whose passion for international affairs allowed us to meet and interview many personalities from around the world. Don Pressley, for his assistance in reaching out and connecting with NGOs worldwide. The Honorable Alexis Lautenberg, ambassador of Switzerland to the UK, for his invaluable input, stimulus, and recommendations while ambassador in Rome. And the Booz Allen Hamilton European Advisory Board for their support and guidance at the beginning of our journey: Didier PineauValencienne, Lord Andrew Turnbull, Lodewick Van Wachem, Claus Helbig, Fedele Confalonieri, Jurgen Harnish, Willy Kissling, and Arne Wittlow.

Gerhard Gschwandtner, publisher of the magazine *Selling Power,* for his encouragement and support in book proposal phase. Laura Graham, for her outstanding support in the final approval for Bill Clinton doing the interview. Clyde E. Williams, Mr. Clinton's domestic policy advisor in his Harlem office, who was instrumental in setting up our interview with the former president; and his wife Mona Sutphen, for her expert counsel on public policy. Stephanie Bell-

Rose, president of the Goldman Sachs Foundation, who was instrumental in getting us the interview with Hank Paulson. Stephen Baum, for all his support and great counsel throughout the process of writing this book.

As we mentioned earlier, this book came to life through a series of conversations with leaders from around the world. While not all interviewees are quoted directly in the book, each contributed significantly to our understanding of the issues, options, and barriers associated with megacommunities. Our sincere thanks to the following leaders who gave so generously of their time, and their insights: Nabil Abadir, director general of the Coptic Evangelical Organization for Social Services; Paul Anderson, Booz Allen Hamilton; José María Aznar, former president of the Spanish government (Prime Minister); MK Bhan, secretary to the government of India, Ministry of Science & Technology/Biotechnology; Ajit Balakrishnan, Rediff.Com India Limited; Leszek Balcerowicz, president of the National Bank of Poland; Charley Beever, Booz Allen Hamilton; Oscar Bernardes, CEO Bunge International; Ian Buchanan, Booz Allen Hamilton; Elio Catania, former chairman & CEO Italian Railways; John Chec, director Esquel Group; Kenneth Chenault, CEO American Express; Linus Cheung, former CEO of Hong Kong Telecom and former vice chairman of PCCW; William Clinton, former president of the United States; Fulvio Conti, CEO Enel SpA; Luca Cordero di Montezemolo, president of Confindustria; Pablo de la Flor, trade minister of Peru; Hernando De Soto, Institute of Liberty and Democracy of Peru; Larry Diamond, senior fellow Hoover Institution, Stanford University; Jean-Jacques Dordain, director General European Space Agency; Dennis Doughty, Booz Allen Hamilton; Peter Eigen, founder, Transparency International; Benita Ferrero-Waldner, European Union Commission; Ian Forbes (Sir), former supreme allied commander, Atlantic (SACLANT) with NATO; Franco Frattini, vice president European Commission; Ann Fudge, chairwoman and CEO Young & Rubicam, Inc.; Sakie Tachibana Fukushima, representative director and president, Korn/Ferry International; Glen S. Fukushima, president and CEO Airbus of Japan; Victor Fung, chairman of Li & Fung; Jacques Gansler, Roger C. Lipitz chair, University of Maryland; George Hara, managing partner Defta Partners; Claus Helbig, Audi Board of Directors and Booz Allen Hamilton Executive Advisory Board member; An Gang Hu, economist/advisor to Chinese Academy of Sciences; Driss Jettou, prime minister, Morocco; Omar Kabbaj, president, African Development Bank; Craig Kennedy, president, The German Marshall Fund; Henry Kissinger, chairman and CEO of Kissinger Associates; Willy Kissling, Unaxis CEO and Booz Allen Hamilton Executive Advisory Board member; Yotaro "Tony" Kobayashi, chairman Fuji-Xerox; Raj Kondur, CEO Nirvana Business solutions; Alexis Lautenberg, Swiss ambassador in London; Paul Leonard, former CEO Habitat for Humanity; Eric Levine, chief executive of Students Partnership Worldwide; Dan Lewis, Booz Allen Hamilton; Justin Yifu Lin, leading economist and advisor to Beijing government; Kaifu Luo, retired chairman of Sinotrans; Cesare Mainardi, Booz Allen Hamilton; Maurizio Mauro, CEO Grupo Abril; Kiran Mazumdar Shaw, CEO Biocon Limited; Aziz Mekouar, Moroccan ambassador to the United States; Steve Merrill, former governor of New Hampshire and president of Bingham Consulting Group; Craig Middleton, vice chairman of Young & Rubicam Brands; Ira M. Millstein, partner, Weil, Gotshal & Manges, LLP; Mario Monti, former European Union Competition commissioner; Jim Morris, executive director, UN World Food Programme; Hiroshi Nakata, mayor of the city of Yokohama; Jim Nicholson, U.S. ambassador; Christine Okerent, France 3 rédaction nationale; Richard Parsons, CEO of Time-Warner; Henry M. Paulson, Jr., former chairman and CEO, Goldman Sachs and secretary of the U.S. Treasury; Susan Penfield, Booz Allen Hamilton; Shimon Peres, MP, Israeli government; Didier Pineau Valencienne, honorary chairman, Schneider Electric and Booz Allen Hamilton Executive Advisory Board member; Roberto Poli, chairman ENI; Don Pressley, Booz Allen Hamilton (former acting director of USAID); Andrea Ragnettie, member of the Group Management Committee of Royal Philips Electronics; Kate Roberts, YouthAIDS; Alan Rosling, Tata Sons; John Ruggie, UN Special Representative for Human Rights and Business and professor at Harvard's Kennedy School of Government; Renato Ruggiero, chairman of Citigroup; Jose T. Sanchez, cardinal Rome Pontifical Academy; Paolo Scaroni, CEO of ENI and former CEO Enel SpA; Otto Schily, interior affairs minister, Germany; John Schubert, chairman of the Commonwealth Bank of Australia; Lucio Stanca, minister of Innovation and Technology, Italy; Seymour Sternberg, chairman and CEO of New York Life Insurance Company; Curt Struble, U.S. Ambassador to Peru; Robert Switz, CEO of ADC Telecommunications Corporation; Marco Tronchetti Provera, former CEO of Telecom Italia; Andrew Turnbull (Lord), former head of the British Civil Service and Cabinet Secretary; Lodewick Van Wachem, chairman, Philips board of directors; Melanne Verveer, chairwoman, Vital Voices; William White, president, Charles Stewart Mott Foundation; Jody Williams, International Campaign to Ban Landmines; Jennifer Windsor, executive director of Freedom House; Arne Wittlow, chairman, Swedish Science Royal Academy and Booz Allen Hamilton Executive Advisory Board member; Jim Woolsey, Booz Allen Hamilton and former CIA Director; Marjorie Yang, chairwoman Esquel Group; George Yong-Boon Yeo, minister of Foreign Affairs Singapore; Dov Zakheim, Booz Allen Hamilton and former undersecretary of Defense (comptroller).

We also have a great editor—Airié Stuart—and her exceptional team of professionals at Palgrave Macmillan, without whom this project would not have been possible.

Working hand-in-hand with Airié has been our own Jon Gage, ensuring that we get things done right and on time. Jon's expertise in publishing has been invaluable as we moved down the path from idea to book. We also thank Deborah Sherman and Debra Storms for their legal expertise in the areas of contracts and intellectual property rights.

Finally, we would like to thank our partners at Booz Allen who have helped us shape this thinking during the past many years. The megacommunity concept is the result of years of experience, and an environment conducive to exploring new ideas. We gained the experience for this concept by working closely with our colleagues worldwide on some of the most challenging projects imaginable. And it is through the collaborative, connected environment that we as a partnership have created—and which uniquely defines Booz Allen—that we are able to explore these important concepts.

ABOUT THE
AUTHORS

Mark J. Gerencser is a senior vice president in Booz Allen Hamilton's global government business, which serves clients in defense, security, and civil government agencies and ministries around the world. Booz Allen Hamilton is a global strategy and technology consulting firm with over $4 billion in annual revenue and more than 19,000 employees.

Mr. Gerencser, who has a BS in electrical engineering from Rutgers University and an MS in technology management from the University of Maryland, joined Booz Allen Hamilton in 1982 as an entry level consultant, and was elected a senior vice president in 2003. Until recently, he served as managing director of the firm's global government business and currently leads the Modeling, Simulation, Wargaming and Analysis Team. Over the past 25 years, he has played a variety of key leadership roles in building the firm's public sector business, as well as in creating its commercial Enterprise Resilience business.

Mr. Gerencser also serves as a member of the firm's Leadership Team which sets the strategic agenda for Booz Allen, including market direction and strategy, resource allocation, and major investments. He serves on Booz Allen's board of directors and is a member of the Personnel Committee. He is the chairman of the Corporate Ethics Committee which oversees ethics and compliance matters across the firm globally.

Mr. Gerencser's has served as a leader on numerous occasions, including leading CEO summits that addressed the interdependencies between business, trade, and security; leading a cyber-summit for *Fortune 1000* and government agency CIOs to create a shared agenda for information privacy and information assurance; chairing several technology studies for the Electronics Industries Association (EIA) to forecast the impact of technological change on business; and representing industry to several Office of Secretary of Defense (OSD) Net Assessment initiatives to help assess the readiness level of U.S. defense capabilities.

He is the founder of the United States National Security Scholarship Program which works with local universities and the federal government to recruit new talent into the National Security Community. He serves on the University of Maryland's Board of Visitors and the Advisory Board for its Strategic Security Laboratory. He is a member of the Royal Institute of International Affairs in the United Kingdom and the Intelligence and National Security Alliance in the United States. *Consulting Magazine* named him one of the top 25 most influential consultants in 2007. Mr. Gerencser has appeared on numerous television news programs (MSNBC, Fox News, CNN) and has been featured in print media as well (*Wall Street Journal, LA Times, Washington Post*). He enjoys golf, snowboarding, and martial arts, and when he is not riding his Harley, you may find him on the diamonds of Northern Virginia coaching youth baseball.

Christopher Kelly is a vice president with Booz Allen and the leader of the Global Security Team which serves clients around the world on issues of homeland security, law enforcement, and national security. Mr. Kelly, who holds both a BS and MS in computer science from Pennsylvania State University, joined Booz Allen as an entry level consultant in 1986. He was elected to vice president in 1997. He is a member of the firm's board of directors and in this role serves on the firm-wide Personnel Committee. His area of professional expertise is in public–private partnerships.

Mr. Kelly tackles issues related to the fragility of the systems we rely on day-to-day to live and work, and how they can be made more resilient in the face of all types of uncertainty. Since joining Booz Allen, Mr. Kelly has worked with all three sectors (government, industry, and civil society) to help develop solutions to a wide range of global dynamic problems. Some examples of his work include defining solutions for law enforcement clients coping with the impact of rapid technology change, government communicators coping with massive regulatory changes in the telecommunications sector and the effect on their emergency communications requirements, and parties coming to grips with the implication of HIV/AIDS prevalence to their citizens, employees, and families. He is currently working on several projects around the world to bring government and industry together to improve the resilience of critical infrastructures in the face of the new twenty-first century threats.

Mr. Kelly has published a number of reports and studies and is also a frequent speaker. He has worked on a global report concerning values-based leadership, which was published in collaboration with the Aspen Institute, and is a contributing member of the study team on critical infrastructure protection led by the Council on Foreign Relations. Mr. Kelly's recent speaking engagements include speaker and facilitator at the World Economic Forum in Davos, the 2006 Aspen Ideas Fest where he chaired a panel on China, India, and Globalization, and at the Brookings Institute in Washington, D.C. where he discussed new approaches to risk management for homeland security. He is a husband of 20 years, and a father of three active kids. He is a little league coach, golfer, avid reader, and enjoys vacationing with his family.

Fernando F. Napolitano is managing partner of Booz Allen Hamilton in Italy. He joined Booz Allen in 1990 and was elected to vice president in 1998. He received his bachelor's degree summa cum laude from Federico II University Business Administration Faculty in Naples, Italy, his MS in technology management from Brooklyn Polytechnic University in New York, and his advanced management program degree from Harvard Business School. Mr. Napolitano coordinates Booz Allen Hamilton's European Advisory Board which is composed of ten leading business personalities from around Europe and chaired by Didier Pineau-Valencienne.

Mr. Napolitano's consulting has focused on competitive strategy, technology, and international competition in the media, telecommunications, and in the aerospace fields. He now specializes on organization and change leadership. Over the last fifteen years, Fernando Napolitano has consulted in more than 30 countries around the world with large industrial and service firms, as well as governments and international organizations. Outside of Booz Allen Hamilton, he has served on the board of directors of Enel SpA, and is also a member of its Compensation Committee. When appointed to Enel's board in 2002, he was the youngest outside director ever appointed to its board. As a board member at Enel, he helped shape to commitment to a megacommunity mindset at the C-suite level and has supported the endowment of a chair at Harvard University—the Enel Endowment for Environmental Economics. This chair is unique in that it is led by the JFK School of Government and involves all ten schools of Harvard University, which will reflect the interdisciplinary nature of the environmental economics.

Mr. Napolitano is a member of the Aspen Institute Italia, member of the Italy-U.S. council that promotes industrial cooperation between the two countries, board member of the American Chamber of Commerce in Italy, and has served on the board of the Italian Aerospace Research Center (CIRA).

Mr. Napolitano is very active within the Italian media community. He has worked as a columnist on international affairs on *Panorama,* the number one Italian weekly business magazine, senior editor for *Panorama Economy,* and a frequent guest on TV networks (such as CNBC) on industrial topics. He has lectured on Italian and European competitive dynamics and written numerous managerial articles on international trade, firm strategy, and global competition. Fernando Napolitano has supported Richard H. K. Vietor, Senator John Heinz Professor of Environmental Management at Harvard Business School, in writing the Business School's first ever country case on Italy in 2000, and recently created a new case for the school in 2007.

Additionally, Mr. Napolitano was also a water-polo player for the Italian national team and a European champion in 1984.

Reginald Van Lee is a senior vice president at Booz Allen Hamilton where he is part of the firm's Organization and Strategy Capabilities Team (which focuses on global health public sector agencies), and also leads the nonprofit business. His expertise lies in understanding how global organizations can build their capabilities to make them resilient to any potential problems that may affect mission accomplishment and growth. He has worked extensively with private sector, public sector, and NGO clients in the area of strategic transformation and high performance organizational design. His experiences are wide-ranging and include redefining business models for global communications, media, and technology companies; co-leading the Urban Enterprise Initiative with the William Jefferson Clinton Foundation in New York City; driving growth and mission accomplishment for nonprofits like Habitat for Humanity, St. Jude's Children's Hospital, the American Cancer Society, and numerous other foundations.

He has coauthored articles on the topic of strategy implementation and developed an innovative and integrated "tool kit" for management with techniques designed to help leaders realize new strategies and institutionalize existing strategies. His article "Rewiring the Corporation" has appeared in the *Journal of Business Strategy* and *Business Horizons*. Mr. Van Lee has also appeared numerous times on ABC's "World News This Morning" and CNBC speaking on the topics of CEO tenures, corporate values, and enterprise resilience.

Mr. Van Lee holds BS and MS degrees from the Massachusetts Institute of Technology. He also earned an MBA at Harvard Business School. Mr. Van Lee is a member and supporter of many organizations and activities outside of Booz Allen Hamilton including the Executive Leadership Council.

Additionally, he is a member of the board of directors of the Thurgood Marshall Scholarship Fund; the Abyssinian Development Corporation, a member of MIT's National Selection Committee; the New York International Ballet Competition; New York City Center for Charter School Excellence; chair of the Board of the EVIDENCE Dance Company; a trustee and treasurer of the Studio Museum in Harlem; and chairman of the Corporate Advisory Board at the University of Southern California's Marshall School of Business. Mr. Van Lee was named one of the top 25 consultants in the world in *Consulting Magazine* in 2000 and recognized as one of New York's finest philanthropists in 2002. In 2004, Mr. Van Lee received New York University's C. Walter Nichols award for outstanding community service, as well as the prestigious Spirit of Cabrini award by the Cabrini Mission Foundation. In 2005, Mr. Van Lee was awarded the Joseph Papp Racial Harmony Award from the Foundation for Ethnic Understanding, and in 2006 he was awarded the Black Engineer of the Year "Pioneer" Award.

NOTES

CHAPTER ONE

1. Douglas Himberger, David Sulek, and Stephen Krill, Jr. "When There Is No Cavalry," *strategy+business* 48 (Autumn 2007).
2. The "Washington Consensus" is a phrase coined by John Williamson to describe a specific set of ten economic policy prescriptions that he considered to constitute a "standard" reform package promoted for crisis-wracked countries by Washington-based institutions such as the International Monetary Fund, World Bank, and U.S. Treasury Department. John Williamson (ed.), *Latin American Readjustment: How Much has Happened* (Washington: Institute for International Economics, 1989).
3. United Nations, "Report of the World Commission on Environment and Development." General Assembly Resolution 42/187, December 11, 1987.
4. Adam Roberts, *Fredric Jameson* (London: Routledge, 2000), p. 140.
5. The 19th-century politician Lord Salisbury complained that the £1.5 million spent on colonial defense by Britain in 1861 merely enabled the nation "to furnish an agreeable variety of stations to our soldiers, and to indulge in the sentiment that the sun never sets on our Empire."
6. Niall Ferguson, *The War of the World: History's Age of Hatred,* (New York: Penguin Press, 2006).
7. Michael D. Bordo, Alan M. Taylor, and Jeffrey G. Williamson (eds) *Globalization in Historical Perspective,* (Chicago: University of Chicago Press, 2003).
8. Gary Fields, "An Ominous Wargame," *The Wall Street Journal,* December 4, 2002.
9. World Trade Organization, Annual Report 2003, February 2003, p. 41.

CHAPTER TWO

1. Steve Stecklow, "Virtual Battle: How a Global Web of Activists Gives Coke Problems in India," *Wall Street Journal,* June 7, 2005, p A–1.
2. Cipla, Ranbaxy Laboratories, Matrix Laboratories, and Hetero Drugs announced an agreement with the Clinton Foundation to provide drugs to four African and nine Caribbean countries at a per capita cost of about $0.37 per day. India's Ministry of

Health, which is still negotiating a final price with the generic drug manufacturers, hopes to obtain the drugs for India at a price even lower than that. *The Washington Quarterly,* (Autumn 2004): p. 8. http://www.twq.com/04autumn/docs/04autumn _mitra.pdf

3. Sam Palmisano, "Multinationals Have Been Superseded," *Financial Times,* June 12, 2006, p. 19.

CHAPTER THREE

1. Henry Chesbrough, Shane Ahern, Megan Finn, and Stephane Guerraz, "Business Models for Technology in the Developing World: The Role of Non-Governmental Organizations," *California Management Review* 48, no. 3 (Spring 2006): pp. 49–50.
2. Randy Starr, Jim Newfrock, Michael Delurey, "Enterprise Resilience–Managing Risk in the Networked Economy," *strategy+business* 30, (Spring 2003).

CHAPTER FOUR

1. BBC News, "Coca-Cola's 'Toxic' India Fertilizer," July 25, 2003. http://edition.cnn/ .com/2003/US/08/15/blackout.glance.ap/index.html.
2. Beth Kytle, Elizabeth Jenkins, and Tamara Bekfi, "CSR Initiative Think Piece: Social Risk as Strategic Risk," July 2006. (Information based on authors' discussion with Doug Daft, former CEO of the Coca-Cola Company, October 18, 2005.)
3. Larry Kahaner, *Competitive Intelligence: How to Gather and Use Information to Move Your Business to the Top* (New York: Simon & Schuster, 1996), p. 17.
4. Environment News Service, "Bird Experts Warn Against Culling Wild Birds to Control Flu," October 20, 2005.
5. Mark Granovetter, "The Strength of Weak Ties," *American Journal of Sociology* 78, no. 6 (May 1973): pp. 1360–1380.

CHAPTER FIVE

1. CNN Travel Destinations, November 11, 1997 http://www.cnn.com/travel/destinations/9711/natural.wonders/
2. For more information on this topic, please see the works of Chris Argyris and Donald Schon, Ellen Langer, Edgar Schein, and Peter Senge.
3. For more information on the International Association of Antarctica Tour Operators (IAATO), please see http://www.iaato.org/guidelines.html
4. Michael E. Porter, *Competitive Advantage: Creating and Sustaining Superior Performance* (New York: Free Press, 1985).
5. "How am I doin'?" was a standard catch phrase of Ed Koch, former New York City mayor from 1978 to 1989.

CHAPTER SIX

1. Art Kleiner, "The Thought Leader Interview: Anne-Marie Slaughter," *strategy+business* 48 (Autumn 2007).

2. Chuck Lucier, Steven Wheeler, and Rolf Habbel, "The Era of the Inclusive Leader," *strategy+business* 47 (Summer 2007).
3. Adapted from Bryan Smith's article in the *Fifth Discipline Fieldbook.*
4. Lucier, Wheeler, and Habbel, "The Era of the Inclusive Leader."

INDEX